ISBN 978-1-331-43219-7
PIBN 10189418

1 MONTH OF
FREE
READING

at
www.ForgottenBooks.com

By purchasing this book you are eligible for one month membership to ForgottenBooks.com, giving you unlimited access to our entire collection of over 1,000,000 titles via our web site and mobile apps.

To claim your free month visit:
www.forgottenbooks.com/free189418

English
Français
Deutsche
Italiano
Español
Português

www.forgottenbooks.com

Mythology Photography **Fiction**
Fishing Christianity **Art** Cooking
Essays Buddhism Freemasonry
Medicine **Biology** Music **Ancient**
Egypt Evolution Carpentry Physics
Dance Geology **Mathematics** Fitness
Shakespeare **Folklore** Yoga Marketing
Confidence Immortality Biographies
Poetry **Psychology** Witchcraft
Electronics Chemistry History **Law**
Accounting **Philosophy** Anthropology
Alchemy Drama Quantum Mechanics
Atheism Sexual Health **Ancient History**
Entrepreneurship Languages Sport
Paleontology Needlework Islam
Metaphysics Investment Archaeology
Parenting Statistics Criminology
Motivational

HIGHLAND TOUR

By ALEX. BEITH, D.D.

STIRLING

SECOND EDITION

EDINBURGH
ADAM AND CHARLES BLACK
1874

Printed by R. & R. CLARK, *Edinburgh.*

NOTICE.

——◆——

THE accompanying Portrait is taken from a drawing made about the year 1843, when Dr. Candlish was in the full vigour of life. The original is in the possession of the Publishers.

CONTENTS.

———◆———

INTRODUCTORY.

CONTENTS.

CONCLUDING DAYS.

INTRODUCTORY.

———◆———

THE General Assembly of the Free Church of Scotland resolved as follows, of date 2d June 1845 :—

"That in the present emergency of the Highlands and Islands, considering how much of the time and attention of the Assembly have been occupied with the affairs of that district of the country, as regards both the oppressive measures adopted against the ministers and members of this Church, and the destitution of the means of grace which prevails ; and further considering that this part of the business of the Assembly cannot be disposed of satisfactorily during their present sittings at Edinburgh,—the General Assembly ought, at its rising in this place, to adjourn, to meet at Inverness on 'Thursday, the 21st of August ensuing, for the purpose of full consultation on the existing state of the Highlands and Islands, with a view to the adoption of such measures as may tend to alleviate the evils under

B

which the Gaelic-speaking population groan, and to promote their spiritual welfare through an adequate supply of the means of grace."

Quite as strong a reason for the *Inverness* Assembly of 1845 could be stated as for the Assembly which had been held in *Glasgow* in the autumn of 1843, which Assembly afforded the precedent for the northern meeting. Two hundred Gaelic-speaking congregations in the Highlands adhered to the Free Church. Nothing like separation from the Established Church had ever before been known; and neither had anything like the bitterly hostile opposition which such separations have always occasioned, ever before been experienced. The southern regions of Scotland had been acquainted with ecclesiastical separations for more than a century. The north had never known any. That which had occurred there recently had proved a great revolution ; and the results following thereon, as indicated by the foregoing resolution of the General Assembly, called for the paternal consideration and interference of the Church at •large. In response to this impression, the *Inverness* Assembly was appointed.

The Free Church has never done things by halves. The reports which from time to time had reached the central authorities were of course credited, and hence the appointment of the *Inverness* Assembly referred to. But it was resolved, preparatory to this "gathering," and with a view to the acquiring of well-authenticated and independent evidence of the state of matters throughout the Highlands and Islands, to adopt definite measures of an official character. Deputations, consisting of members of Assembly and a few others, both ministers and elders, were nominated, whose duty it became to visit the respective districts of the North, that, by personal observation and special inquiries, they might become well instructed in all matters requiring the interference of the Church, and that when, at the close of their respective tours, they appeared at the grand *rendezvous*, they might be furnished with information which could not be gainsaid, and which might enable the Assembly to adjudicate rightly in all questions claiming their attention.

I was asked to prepare, and to submit to a Committee in charge of the arrangements, a scheme of the route which each deputation respectively, should have assigned to it, the places which they should visit, and the steps which they should adopt with a view to the contemplated object.

My scheme, with some modifications, was approved of, and three deputations were named. The details of the arrangements connected with the progress of *one* of these only, I undertook. Even this limited duty was onerous, for it involved extensive correspondence previous to the departure of the deputation, and not less so during its journeyings. It required that those residing in the localities intended to be visited should be advertised of our approach ; that their acceptance of our proposed visits should be ascertained ; that day and hour, as well as place of meetings, should be arranged ; that means of conveyance should be provided for, to prevent delay and disappointment ; and that necessary accommodation should not be to seek when the deputation arrived at the various stages assigned to it. This done, it still remained that all concerned should, statedly, after our journeyings began, be reminded of what had been arranged, lest forgetfulness or misunderstanding should, practically, frustrate our supposed well-laid plans.

The deputation with which I was connected was directed to the West Highlands and Islands, and Dr. M‘Kellar and Dr. Candlish were my colleagues. The ground which we traversed, and the work which we accomplished, will appear in the sequel. Perhaps I may be permitted to sketch shortly each of my distinguished associates, as they always, and especially on this interesting occasion, impressed me.

Dr. M'Kellar was, like myself, an Argyleshire Highlander. The accent peculiar to our county he had, and to the last retained, in perfection. To my ear it was always grateful, whatever it may have been to others.

Dr. M'Kellar was a man of fine personal appearance ; not a large man, and not a little man ; but elegant in form and in manners. His bearing and style, without being in the least affected, were highly polished. His natural temper was of the sweetest. His literary attainments were far above the average. His eloquence, without being in the least florid, was correct, tasteful, manly, expressive, and effective. He was not a forward man, but he never failed to take, in Church courts and on public occasions, the place to which all held him to be entitled. If not of the "first three," he certainly was of the "thirty." His good sense never failed him ; and few of our public men more effectually guided the opinions of the younger brethren than he.

I had always the deepest respect for this good man. He was not brilliant, he was not profound : but he was not in the least commonplace. · On the contrary, he never rose to speak, but you might expect to hear from him views full of instruction and wisdom. It was no wonder that such a man was called to occupy the chair of the Moderator of the General Assembly. Twice this honour was conferred upon him ; *first*, a few years before the Disruption, when the conflict was running high, and the *second* time, after the Disruption, when we had passed through our stormy sea, and were floating happily on still waters. Of all the Moderators I have seen in the chair, during more than fifty years, there has been no one I would compare to Dr. M'Kellar as he appeared in that capacity in his pre-Disruption tenure of office. He was a pattern in all respects. His post-Disruption moderatorship was good too ; but the times had changed, and afforded little opportunity, comparatively, for the exercise of the graces which distinguished him. Moreover, he was then an older man than on the first occasion, and the vigour necessary for carrying a man in high effectiveness through such duties as he had to discharge, was then somewhat abated. The *stateliness* of past times had greatly disappeared in the Church disestablished, and, with that, one of the elements in which Dr. M'Kellar excelled—nay, which, I may say, he graced. On both occasions, however, he was a most popular Moderator. His composure and tact were the same. So was his perfect impartiality; his patience with senselessness and bad manners; his courteous bearing amidst the brusque impetuosity which marked some of our leading men both before and after the Disruption, but more after than before—brushing aside, as it did, the dignified orderliness of earlier times; and, finally, his uniformly encouraging kindness to the younger members, who essayed to introduce themselves to the "fathers and brethren," in delivering their maiden speeches in the great Assembly.

I need scarcely say that Dr. M'Kellar had always been attached to the Evangelical party in the Establishment. My earliest recollections of him, as a preacher, are connected with the seasons, during my first years as a student at the Glasgow University, when, on communion occasions, he used to assist Dr. Balfour in the OUTER HIGH. It must have been in the spring of 1814 that I heard him preach there on John xiv. 1—"Let not your heart be troubled," etc.—a sermon, the pleasing effect of which I remember even now,—so long a time after hearing it.

In the private circle—in domestic life—he was a pleasing example of urbanity and kindliness. Blessed with a partner (one of the daughters of

Keir) distinguished, no less than himself, by the
graces of cultivated and refined life, it was a privilege which I at all times highly valued to partake of
the hospitalities of his family, which I had often
the happiness to do. I look back to those occasions
with a lively recollection of the pleasure they afforded
me, and of the benefit which they conferred on me.

Such is my description of one of the friends with
whom I had the honour of being associated in this
journey. Am I to describe the other? Is he
describable? Ought any man to undertake to set
Dr. Candlish before the mind's eye by any attempted
sketch? If I do attempt it, I must do so from
the standpoint of thirty years ago, and chiefly for
those who have not had the happiness of seeing
or knowing this honoured man. If in such an
attempt contrast affords special advantage—that
is, the opportunity of setting your subject side
by side with his opposite in what may be describable in both—then I enjoy that advantage,
having before me, on the one hand, my venerable
friend, and on the other the distinguished leader in
the great non-intrusion and Free Church history.

For elegance in form and manner in Dr.
M'Kellar, we had a diminutive person, though
every inch of it manly, in Dr. Candlish. For
readiness to give way to others in the one, we had

promptitude and a most willing offering of himself to show and to lead the way, on occasions of diffi-culty, in the other. For the steady pace of the well-trained *cob* in the first, we had the impetuous dash of the fiery *Arab* in the other. If Dr. M'Kellar's natural temper was such that he never needed to bridle himself, but, obeying his natural tendencies, always acted decorously, Dr. Candlish's natural temper was of a character requiring the strong will, which in him was a power, so to keep him within limits that he never failed to *appear* what Dr. M'Kellar really was. If Dr. M'Kellar was not brilliant, Dr. Candlish was eminently so, especially in pre-Disruption times, when he shone as a star of the first magnitude. If Dr. M'Kellar stood high, comparatively, as to social position, and perhaps piqued himself a little on it, Dr. Candlish occupied no such place, and, if he had, would not have cared one jot for it. Finally, if Dr. M'Kellar was the very pink of neatness in dress as well as person, never appearing, either in public or private, but as if he had come fresh from his clothier's, Dr. Candlish, with exceptional occasions due to circumstances, which came like angels' visits, appeared as if, in making his toilette, he had mistaken the dress of another for his own ; or as if he had shot his person into his own dress, not caring nor considering whether the articles which composed it were put on straight or awry ; or whether, when adorned after his fashion, his appearance should excite either admiration or amusement. If Dr. M'Kellar was of the " Thirty," beyond all doubt Dr. Candlish was of the " First Three."

My two associates had, nevertheless, much in common. They were both noble by nature, of cultivated mind, of good scholarship ; most unselfish, generous, good ; the servants of the same Master ; the honest advocates of the same great principles of truth. They were warm friends. Dr. M'Kellar loved Dr. Candlish with the affection of a father for a son. He chose him as his minister when he himself ceased to preach, and he became one of his kirk-session in Free St. George's. Dr. Candlish, I know, felt towards Dr. M'Kellar as a revered father ; never altered in his regard for him ; soothed his deathbed by affectionate attentions ; and, when the venerable man was carried to the " long home," and laid in the " narrow house appointed for all living," poured out from the pulpit a touching eulogy, which could have had no other origin than honest and earnest Christian love.

It was no small privilege to be associated, as I was at this time, with two such men.

I MET Dr. Candlish.in Glasgow. From that point we started on our mission. It was on the 29th day of July. Dr. M'Kellar did not join us until we had reached Oban. Our first stage was *Islay*, whither we proceeded by steamboat from West Tarbert. The weather was remarkably fine, and, though our ship was a mere tub, going no more than six miles an hour, the voyage, in crossing the channel from the Kintyre coast, was very delightful. Our arrival at Port Ellen was expected, and no small commotion was thereby excited among the Free Church community, as well as among the party opposed to them, who bore them but little good will.

Mr. Walter Campbell, nephew of the Duke of Argyll, and long M.P. for Argyleshire, was, at the time of our visit, proprietor of all Islay, with the exception of one or two small portions of the island, which were possessed by others. He was at home. On our arrival his factor came on board, dressed in full Highland costume, and delivered hospitable messages from his superior. This was kindly meant. We fully appreciated the compliment paid to us. But as our time was limited and our business urgent, we could do no more than call for the chieftain at the stately mansion-house of his noble property. Alas, that it should have so soon passed from him! At the time of our visit, as we learned afterwards, he was close to a painful discovery which, it was said, was to him as unexpected as it was unwelcome— a discovery of his utter insolvency! In politics he was a Liberal, and, with all classes, he was a very popular man.

Mr. Campbell's horses, with one of his equipages, were placed at our disposal. The journeyings we had to perform in fulfilling the purposes of our mission made this very much a favour, and we thankfully availed ourselves of it. Our drive along the sands on the margin of *Lochindal*, and into the district of the island which we visited, was charming. In going the tide was at low ebb; in returning it was in full flood, so that the beauty of the drive, under both conditions, was enjoyed by us. We addressed meetings at the church of Kilmeny, as well as at Port Ellen, where I preached. Small matters which called for interference were easily arranged. Our authority in dealing with them was not called in question; our adjudication was thankfully accepted, and the good which we effected proved permanent. We passed one night only on the island, making our abode with Mr. Ramsay, of Kildalton, and partaking of his generous hospitality.

The condition of the Free Church in this quarter we found to be very satisfactory. Both Proprietor, and factor, Mr. Cheyne, favoured it, so setting an example, worthy to be imitated, and affording a practical protest against all oppressive site-refusers and persecutors in various forms, in other parts of the Highlands.

We left *Islay*, as we had come there, by aid of steam. Our voyage, in returning, was not so protracted as it had been in going. As our intention was to proceed to *Campbeltown*, some thirty miles off from the opening into Loch Tarbert, we landed from the steamer at the nearest point to the high road. There a conveyance, which my brother John, Provost of the burgh, had sent for us, awaited our arrival, and by it we proceeded comfortably on our journey. Late in the evening we reached the capital of *Kintyre*, and were most kindly welcomed. We were my brother's guests. Our day's journey had not been all our work. At *Killean*, some eighteen miles from Campbeltown, a Free Church congregation had, to the surprise of many, been formed. We were expected to call there. Dr. Candlish, in his usual generous manner, readily consented to do so, that we might encourage the people, and that we might show such respect as we could to the promising young minister under whose charge the flock then was. Mr. Clark did not long survive our visit. Early death removed him from amongst us, and deprived the church of a very estimable servant of the Lord Jesus. The day became very tempestuous. The place of meeting, in which the congregation worshipped Sabbath after Sabbath, was perched on the top of a hill, terribly exposed—looking down on the surging sea of the wide Atlantic, the sound of whose roaring waves the ecclesiastical erection did not exclude on that day. The erection consisted of a canvas tent upheld by poles, and fastened to the soil by wooden pins, to which its cords were attached. To this primitive tabernacle, through the sweep of the tempest of wind and rain, we made our way. Had it collapsed, had it fallen down on us, no one could have been surprised. Happily we had no such adventure; though the undulations of the cloth and the creaking of the wood in the erection were by no means assuring. Dr. Candlish addressed this interesting congregation, which had assembled notwithstanding the inclemency of the weather, in English. I preached to them in the Gaelic tongue. Both minister and people expressed deep gratitude, and we felt assured that they were comforted. As for me, I was here in the land of my fathers—in the country, and district of country, in which they had been 'known for generations, and had been witnesses for truth in evil times. Once before (in 1821), soon after I became a minister, I had preached in *Killean*, then in the parish church; now I did so on the hill-side, in testimony of adherence to principles which had ever been precious in Scotland — adherence to which had not now for the first time entailed sacrifice and suffering.

At *Campbeltown* everything went well with us. The community were gratified by the visit of Dr. Candlish, of whom they had heard so much, and whose great efforts in the cause of truth they were so well able to appreciate. Here, nearly a century previous to the time of our visit, conflicts of a very arduous character for spiritual liberty had taken place. Abuse of the law of patronage had occasioned it. All redress being, in the high-handed manner of the times, refused with scorn, the patriots of the occasion separated themselves from the Establishment, and, after encountering and

overcoming such resistance and persecution at the
hands of lairds and civil authority as came to be
too well known in our Free Church times, succeeded in erecting for themselves a place of worship, where, as Seceders, they exercised the right,
as they had manfully fought for it, of worshipping
God according to the light of conscience, and in
the enjoyment of the liberty with which Christ had
made them free. At *Campbeltown*, therefore, the first
separation from the State Church in Argyleshire,
and indeed in all the Western Highlands, took place.
From the first this seceding congregation was a great
power, asserting the principle of spiritual liberty in a
land where such assertion implied an amount of
moral hardihood the value of which cannot, at the
present era, be understood or appreciated. The
Campbeltown Relief congregation was a phenomenon of its kind. It was soon joined by a consort
in the neighbourhood, whose existence had the same
origin. But the Campbeltown congregation always
held the first place in the district, and, till this day,
is counted to be among the foremost of the congregations of the great United Presbyterian Church
of Scotland.

All honour, which circumstances permitted, was
done to Dr. Candlish in Campbeltown. One day
was all the time which we could afford for this my

native town. A public dinner was proposed, with the view of testifying regard for the distinguished visitor. The services which were required from us in the evening forbade the accepting of such a testimony. But a public breakfast was accepted. This was held in the Town Hall, where a large assemblage convened. A pleasant time was enjoyed. Dr. Candlish made more than one speech, whilst in all the addresses delivered by others on the occasion many compliments were paid to him, and he received the hearty expression of earnest good will.

The services of the evening were on a large scale. As introductory, I was required to preach. The public meeting followed. At it Dr. Candlish was, of course, the chief speaker. The great topic was the deliverance accomplished by the Church from the thraldom of the civil courts, which had so ruinously interfered with spiritual action in the obedience due to the Head in Heaven, first, in the matter of the people's right to choose their own ministers and office-bearers; and second, with regard to the Church's exclusive allegiance to Him in the service of the gospel generally. Dr. Candlish's statement was distinguished by all his usual clearness, force, and elegance. The impression produced was great, and all the more for the practical use

c

which, with a view to the edification of his hearers, he made of the principles which he had expounded, and of the circumstances resulting in our relief from State connection, and, consequently, State control.

So much work awaited us that we were not allowed to remain together during the Sabbath at *Campbeltown*. One of us must needs preach at *Inveraray*, at the other extremity of the county. Dr. Candlish had been selected for this duty ; and, accordingly, on Saturday (August 2) he took his departure to fulfil the engagement. I remained to preach at *Campbeltown*. With these services the first week of our tour terminated. The weeks which followed were marked by events more numerous and more unusual ; but the results of what we had, in the few days now past, aecomplished, were important to the cause which we aimed at serving. Those whom we had visited and addressed were pleased and gratified, whilst much information had been obtained and recorded for the purposes of the deputation.

SECOND WEEK.

On Monday Dr. Candlish, after his Sabbath's work at Inveraray, came to *Tarbert*, on Lochfine-side. There I met him, having that morning come from *Campbeltown*. Our destination that day, in prosecuting our work, was *Lochgilphead*, where we had been announced for services in the evening. The services, accordingly, were held. In the first instance, I preached in Gaelic to a crowded audience redolent of the flavour of fresh herrings. It was impossible not to feel that we were amidst a crowd of hardy and intelligent fishermen, ready to receive, and qualified to appreciate, the things which we had to say to them. Dr. Candlish was very happy in his English address. What had impressed me in *Islay* still more impressed me at *Lochgilphead*—his wonderful skill in speaking with a simplicity of expression which made all that he said intelligible, even when the knowledge of English on the part of his hearers was very scanty. In all our tour, on every occasion on which he addressed Highlanders, if the least knowledge of English was possessed by them, they declared themselves delighted, maintained that they understood him, and that his English was different from that of their own (Highland) ministers. Theirs they could not follow : his they did. Everywhere therefore they remained, when the Gaelic service was ended, to listen to his English address. This was notably the case at *Lochgilphead*, where the adhesion to the Free Church had been very extensive, and where enthusiasm in the cause was great.

Reflecting on this, I could not but recall the memory of an early and beloved friend, who was the first minister settled in this village. I refer to PETER M'KICHAN. *Lochgilphead* was one of the " Government charges," as they were denominated, —not an original parish, and not a chapel-of-ease, but a *quoad sacra* charge—erected, furnished with church and manse, and endowed by the Government, who retained in their own hands the right of patronage in the case of all *livings* of this class. Mr. M'Kichan had, as a student of divinity, been, along with his father's family, of my congregation at *Oban* from 1821 until my removal to Hope Street Chapel, Glasgow, in 1824. When consulted by the local proprietor, Mr. M'Niel of *Oakfield*, who was permitted by Government to name a minister for the new charge, I had no difficulty in recommending for his selection my friend Mr. M'Kichan. . In due time he was ordained over the flock, which, though at its beginnings small, soon grew, under his very acceptable ministerial efforts, to a large and influential congregation.

Mr. M'Kichan was an attractive man, who, with few pretensions, exercised extensive influence. Of mild and gentle manners, endowed with a persuasive eloquence, thoroughly instructed in the great truths of evangelical doctrine, well read on all subjects, earnest, loving, energetic, he was as a minister of the Lord Jesus beloved by all who knew him, and, in his time, was greatly honoured as an instrument of good in all the neighbourhood in which we now were. I do not know that he took an active part in the effort made to rouse the country to a sense of the urgency of the crisis which resulted in the separation of what is now the Free Church from the State. It was then felt to be of the first importance that the people of Scotland should be made fully aware of the great change about to take place in our relative position, as a Church, to the Government of the country—a change forced upon us by the oppressive measures of the State, and which we were absolutely shut up to, unless, indeed, we consented to abandon our liberty to carry on the work of the ministry in obedience to the law of the gospel, and as fulfilling the mind of Christ. · But whether Mr. M'Kichan took much part in this work of agitation or not he entirely approved of it. His influence was all employed on the side of those who did. His own people were thoroughly educated in the questions which were discussed at this time, and, when the day of decision came, no part of the Highlands afforded more unequivocal evidence of intelligence as to the truths which were maintained, or of resolution to stand by· them at all hazards. Mr. M'Kichan did not see the Disruption. Though he avoided the more exciting efforts to which the ministry generally were called, in view of the approaching catastrophe, the subject had a deep hold of his mind—perhaps all the deeper hold, that he was more a witness of the great struggle than an actor in it. An attack of brain fever ensued, under which he lingered for a time, and then was taken away to the land where such strife as that to which we on earth were constrained is unknown; for " there the wicked cease from troubling," and the weary get rest.

The prosperous state of matters at *Lochgilphead* I trace, I believe on good grounds, to the influence of my early friend. I may be permitted to add that I trace the same also, very much, to the influence of my honoured father, who, for fifty years nearly, was, in this locality, a bold and uncompromising advocate of evangelical truth in evil times, and who, from his qualifications of mind, as well as his social position, was trusted and followed as a guide and as an example in those questions, which led to the breaking up of the Church of Scotland in 1843.

The morning which followed our evening services at *Lochgilphead* saw Dr. Candlish and myself at *Ardrishaig*, two miles to the south of Lochgilphead, at the inlet to the Crinan Canal, awaiting the swift steamer from Glasgow. By her came Dr. Begg, member of another deputation —one of those which had been commissioned on similar work to ours, by the late Assembly, though in a different region. His colleagues were Dr. M'Kay, late of Harris, and Mr. Glass, late of Musselburgh. Dr. M'Kay joined him at Oban, Mr. Glass at a more advanced point in our tour. Dr. Begg was the companion of Dr. Candlish and myself for the day. The romantic pass from Lochfine, on the east shore of the vast peninsula of Kintyre, to Crinan on the west, never looked more beautiful than on this day, and never was looked on by more admiring eyes. My two associates were in their happiest moods — Dr. Candlish as joyous as a boy on vacation from school—Dr. Begg overflowing with humour and anecdote; of the latter it seemed as if there could be no end. As for myself, I was in the district in which I had been brought up. Every point in the landscape was familiar to me, and I was able to communicate to my fellow-travellers incidents of interest, bearing date for fifty years previous to the time of our journey, connected with this district. Every new turn in our progress suggested reminiscences, some joyous, some sad; and as my friends seemed willing to listen, I did not refrain my speech, but trespassed perhaps on their good nature, or on their good manners, more than I ought to have done.

How comes it that when, in advanced life, we visit scenes which were familiar to us in childhood—scenes which, in the interval, we may frequently have visited—we recur, with deepest feeling, to impressions which were produced at the early period? For my part, even till this day, when I visit *Lochgilphead* and the neighbourhood, my mind recurs to the times when I believed that the sky rested on the hills which surround the village, and that if I were able to reach their summit I should behold the limits of the earth—the times when I had no convictions as to the existence of a world beyond that on which my childish eyes then looked. How comes this? and what makes the illusion so pleasing when such impressions are reproduced?

The early evening brought our party to OBAN, the scene of the first days of my ministry. Twenty-four years before the period of this visit I was the youthful, and I may add, the hard-working minister of OBAN. Already the bulk of those who had then formed my flock were gone; few remained of those who once knew me—so rapidly does the flight of time bring changes; so soon does it come to pass that the places which knew us, know us not. I was not quite so much a stranger here as my associates in our present service, yet I did feel myself more a stranger than I cared to be.

We had passed, in our romantic sail from *Crinan* through the slate isles, the parish of Kibrandon, where, for about four years from 1826, I had been minister. In the distance, to the east, as we sped along towards the north, the old parish church, on the shore of the *Cuan*, was visible. I pointed it out to my friends. The rapidity of the tide, as it rushes through this strait, narrowed by the projecting shores of the island of *Seil* on the one hand, and of *Luing* on the other, always great, is sometimes quite terrific.

It was often a cheering sight to witness on the

Sabbath morning the vast fleet of large slate-makers' boats, from the islands of *Easdale* and *Ellanabeach*, crowded with men, women, and children, coming to attend church, sweep through this pass, floating on the raging tide, scarcely needing the use of oars but to guide their course—no return being possible until the *ebbing* waters had become exhausted, and until, changing their course, they came back in full *flood*, to carry home again, with an equally small expense of toil, the crowds which in the interval had worshipped in the temple of God. Alternately the parishioners of the eastern portions of my charge enjoyed this advantage, when those from the other side then required to travel by the road.

The services at *Oban* were conducted by Dr. Candlish and Dr. Begg. We had no admission to the church, although it had been erected, in 1821, very much by my own efforts. I had collected money for the work in London, and all over Scotland, in times when the virtue of GIVING was but little practised—giving, I mean, for such objects as church-building. Indeed, I bestowed much labour on this Oban church, once not a little famed for the controversy to which it gave rise, conducted on the one side by Dr. Wardlaw of Glasgow, and on the other by Mr. Carment, then of the same city; but, though once having absolute control over it, now I could have the use of it neither for my friends nor for myself. So do times change, and so do the former things pass away.

The schoolroom had been preserved for the Free Church in the wreck occasioned by the Disruption. There we held our meeting;—an enthusiastic meeting. Though no part of our purpose in coming to this locality, yet it suggested itself to us that the occasion might be employed for originating a movement for the erection of a Free Church. This was done; and, at the close of our present services, a considerable sum was subscribed by the friends who were present. What was thus happily begun made comfortable progress. The powerful aid of the late lamented Marquess of Breadalbane came, in due time, to the furtherance of the object. The result was the handsome church, manse, and other accommodations, which now occupy so conspicuous a place amidst the romantic environs of this elegant town.

Next day was devoted to recreation. Dr. M'Kellar and Dr. M'Kay had joined us, so that the members of two deputations, with the exception of Mr. Glass, had met. Our recreation for the day was to be the circumnavigating of the island of Mull by the steamer which statedly pursued that route. Our course lay through the Sound of *Kerrara*, the channel between the island so named and *Mull*; by the west of Mull to Iona and Staffa; thence to Tobermory; and back to our starting-point, through the Sound of Mull, past the southern extremity of the island of *Lismore*. We anticipated a day of enjoyment,—such a route— such company—and amidst the finest weather!

Feeling a sort of responsibility for at least one of the deputations represented in the present assemblage, I was the first-arrived of the party at the pierhead, where our steamer lay, sending forth from funnel and steam valves, indescribable by me, noises the harshest and most ear-rending—panting for relief, as it appeared, relief that could come only with permission given to go forth on her course, to plough her way through the yielding flood. I became impatient; I knew, however, that captain, hands, and all, were aware what one portion of their freight for the day was to be; and I felt sure that some egregious shortcoming must occur on our side if any of our party were ultimately left behind.

My friends came—not being chargeable with any culpable delay. First Dr. M'Kellar appeared, slowly advancing, neatly dressed, showing snow-white linens, carefully brushed hat and greatcoat, and (conspicuous beyond all the rest) a rich, blushing, beautiful bouquet in his hand—how acquired, or where, was to me a mystery. Next in order came Dr. Candlish, whose pace was not so measured as that of our honoured senior member, and who, catching sight of the bouquet, made many sportive efforts, on coming up to its possessor, to get it into his own hands. All life and sprightliness, he formed a contrast to the other constituents of our group; but, at the same time, inspired us all with a measure of his spirit, and created by his cheerful demeanour a happy commencement of our day's excursion. There was a great deal of talking on all hands as we approached the ship, and, both on shore and on board, we became, very much, the observed of all observers.

The route of the excursion of this day of pleasure was not new to me. A quarter of a century before I had visited the interesting seat of CULDEE literature for which we were bound—of Culdee faithful testimony and fervent devotedness to God —as well as the marvellous natural pile of the island of Staffa. Neither Iona nor Staffa was, therefore, now to me a sight so striking as they both had been on my seeing them for the first time; for when you have once seen those islands, form-

ing such contrasts to each other in their natural
appearance, all subsequent visits are thereby made
comparatively less affecting, inasmuch as the
memory and imagination never lose first impressions of them, and never cease to recall those, magnifying them when they do.

The following account, by Montalembert, in his
"Monks of the West," of the line of coast along
which we this day sailed, cannot fail to be read
with interest, as it must ever supersede all other
descriptions :—"He who has not seen the islands
and gulfs of the western coast of Scotland, and who
has not been tossed upon the sombre sea of the
Hebrides, can scarcely form any image of it to
himself. Nothing can be less seductive at the
first glance than that austere and solemn nature,
which is picturesque without charm, and grand
without grace. The traveller passes sadly through
an archipelago of naked and desert islands, sowed
like so many extinct volcanoes upon the dull and
sullen waters, which are broken by rapid currents and
dangerous whirlpools. Except on rare days, when
the sun—that pale sun of the North—gives life to
these shores, the eye wanders over a vast surface
of gloomy sea, broken at intervals by the whiten-
ing crest of waves, or by the foaming line of the
tide, which dashes here against long reefs of rock,

there against the immense cliffs, with a forlorn roar which fills the air. Through the continual fogs and rains of that rude climate may be seen by times the summits of chains of mountains, whose abrupt and naked sides slope to the sea, and whose base is bathed by these cold waves which are kept in constant agitation by the shock of contrary currents, and the tempests of wind which burst from the lakes and narrow ravines farther inland. The melancholy of the landscape is relieved only by that peculiar configuration of the coast, which has been remarked by the ancient authors, and especially by Tacitus—a configuration which exists besides only in Greece and Scandinavia. As in the fiords of Norway, the sea cuts and hollows out the shores of the islands into a host of bays and gulfs of strange depth, and as narrow as profound. These gulfs take the most varied forms, penetrating by a thousand tortuous folds into the middle of the land, as if to identify themselves with the long and winding lakes of the Highland interior. Numberless peninsulas, terminating in pointed headlands, or summits covered with clouds; isthmuses so narrow as to leave the sea visible at both sides; straits so closely shut between two walls of rock, that the eye hesitates to plunge into that gloom; enormous

cliffs of basalt or of granite, their sides perforated
with rents ; caverns, as at Staffa, lofty as churches,
flanked through all their length by prismatic columns, through which the waves of the ocean dash
with groans ; and here and there, in contrast with
that wild majesty, perhaps on an island, perhaps
upon the shore of the mainland, a sandy beach, a
little plain, covered with scanty, prickly grass, a
natural port capable of sheltering a few frail boats ;
everywhere, in short, a strangely varied combina-
tion of land and sea, but where the sea carries the
day, penetrates and dominates everything. . . .
Such is the present aspect.   Such must have been,
with the addition of the forests which have disappeared, the aspect of these shores when Columba
sought them to continue and end his life there."

Our entire party landed at *Iona*.   Not so at
Staffa.   By the time we arrived off that isle,
though the sun still shone with all brightness, the
sea had risen considerably.   The captain of our
ship doubted whether he could, with perfect
safety, send his boat to the rocky shore.   He certainly could promise no comfort to those who
wished to land in doing so.   As to rowing into
Fingal's Cave, it could not be attempted.   Urged
somewhat, he launched his landing-boat.   Dr.
Candlish was among the first to spring into it.

The party with difficulty succeeded in setting foot on shore, where they were able, not without peril, however, to look into the cave, and so to judge of its sublime magnitude. This was all. It required the enthusiasm of their admiration to reconcile them to the drenching by the sea spray which they had encountered in their adventure.

We returned from Iona and Staffa *via* TOBERMORY, that beautiful bay which has so often proved a haven of safe shelter for the ocean-tossed ships of the wild Atlantic, and whose waters no tempest, however terrific, can at any time touch.

> " Est in secessu longo locus : insula portum
> Efficit objectu laterum, quibus omnis ab alto
> Frangitur inque sinus scindit sese unda reductos.
> Hinc atque hinc vastae rupes geminique minantur
> In coelum scopuli, quorum sub vertice late
> Aequora tuta silent : tum silvis scena coruscis
> Desuper horrentique atrum nemus imminet umbrâ."
>
> *Æneid,* Lib. i. 159-65.

> " Within a long recess there lies a bay :
> An island shades it from the rolling sea,
> And forms a port secure for ships to ride ;
> Broke by the jutting land, on either side,
> In double streams the briny waters glide
> Betwixt two rows of rocks : a sylvan scene
> Appears above, and groves for ever green :
> A grot is formed beneath, with mossy seats,
> To rest the Nereids and exclude the heats."
>
> *Dryden's Translation.*

D

Searching for this harbour, and not finding it, many of the ships of the Spanish Armada were wrecked at no great distance from its entrance. Few of those embarked on board the ill-fated transports escaped. Some did, and their descendants, both in Mull and on the adjacent coast to the north, may yet be traced among the native population. The Mull riding-ponies are, or were, considered the finest in Scotland. Their superior quality was supposed to have been occasioned from the breed of the native Highland horses being improved by the mixture of Spanish horse blood, through the animals which escaped, and in the frightful shipwreck on this iron-bound coast more than three hundred years ago, found their way to the shore. The only relic of the great catastrophe I have seen anywhere in the West Highlands, was a brass gun of no great size, which, in my time, had found a resting-place on the summit of the ruined wall of Dunstaffnage Castle. Approaching, in point of dimensions, the Armstrong gun, it could have none of the power of that deadly weapon of war.

At Tobermory, Dr. M'Kellar and Dr. M'Kay embarked on board the BREADALBANE yacht, a part of our Free Church ecclesiastical machinery for prosecuting evangelistic work in the Highlands and Islands. Their destination was *Loch Sunart, Ardnamurchan, Ballachulish,* and the surrounding country. Dr. Begg, accompanied by the minister of Tobermory and an elder from Oban, took his route for *Ardnamurchan* proper and the adjoining districts. Dr. Candlish and I, again left by ourselves, proceeded to Fort-William, passing through the Sound of *Mull,* having *Morven* and the *Kingairloch* mountains on our left, through a magnificently sunenlightened course, first towards the east to Oban, and thence northwards to the place of our destination. On the day following our arrival at *Fort-William,* accompanied by the two ministers of this district, we passed from *Fort-William* to *Kilmally.* There I preached in the Gaelic tongue. After being occupied for the day in arranging certain matters connected with the district, and helping, by counsel, those who needed it, we retraced our steps to *Fort-William.* There I again preached in Gaelic. Dr. Candlish preached in English. We had large congregations, and were occupied, after our pulpit work, for some time with business of the same description as we had transacted during the forenoon on the opposite side of the plain. A second night's repose at *Fort-William* was required to prepare us for the adventures of the succeeding day.

It was a day, the remembrance of which has

often, since, awakened feelings both of an indignant, and, though the contrast may seem inconsistent, ludicrous character.

I have already noted that, before we started from home on our excursion, as it became one to whom the details of the arrangements were committed, I had corresponded with all the persons with whom it was necessary to communicate, with a view to facilitate our progress, and to prevent disappointment either to ourselves or to those who expected our approach along the line by which we were to pursue our journey in fulfilling our mission. Assuring myself of our punctuality, if health permitted and Providence favoured us, our beds were everywhere engaged, as well as our places in coaches and by other modes of conveyance, indubitable evidence of which I took care to have in my possession. Nothing was left to the efforts which we might, or might not, successfully make at the various points of arrival when we reached them. All was arranged weeks before.

Among other pre-arrangements, I had corresponded with the coach-office at *Fort-William*, and had secured two seats on the top of the coach running to *Inverness*. I had secured them for the morning of Friday, with the provision that we should be set down at *Invergarry*, the first stage, although a long one, on the way to Inverness ; our purpose being to travel by *Invergarry, Tomandoun, Cluny,* and *Shielhouse,* to *Glenelg,* where we were to meet the steamer from *Glasgow* and the south, to carry us on to *Lochalsh* and *Skye.* I had corresponded with mine host of *Invergarry* Inn (an old friend), and I had engaged his only spring-vehicle and good-going horse, to carry us thus on our way to Glenelg. In short, I had prepared for our being conveyed to my old parish church there, under the walls of which we were, on the Saturday morning, by a given hour, to take boat, that we might embark on board the steamer.

When we arrived at *Fort-William* I immediately repaired to the coach-office, paid for our tickets, received them from the clerk, and made all sure, offering at the same time to pay for the seats all the way through to *Inverness,* if crowding of the coach were apprehended, or should make that necessary. I requested that that should be noted, which was done. I feared nothing, and believed that I needed not to fear. Date and all was right. No difficulty was made on any hand.

It was now the Friday of our second week. Much depended on punctuality marking our course for this day. Dr. Candlish never failed in that virtue, and was never behind. This morning he

was up betimes. We had breakfast, and, being
.all ready, when the coach drew up we at once
took our places, he on the box seat beside the
driver, I on the one immediately behind, all snug,
with our traps safely stowed in the " boot."

The day was beautiful. We had every prospect
of a delightful journey. Eleven o'clock at latest
would see us at *Invergarry* Inn. The conveyance,
as promised,. ready for us there, we should push
on, and, by my calculation, arrive at Glenelg in
the evening. The coach was soon occupied—in-
side, outside, every side. Why did the coachman
not proceed? We were impatient. Some one was
expected. But who could be expected, seeing the
coach was full to overflowing—every place occupied—more places than ought to have been occupied? Who could be expected? Our questioning
was soon answered. Dr. Robert Lee of Edinburgh
approached, accompanied by a friend and the proprietor of the coach. We had not seen him previously.

In the "Life and Remains of Robert Lee, D.D.,"
by Dr. Story, minister of Roseneath, the following account of the incident to which I am referring
occurs :—

"At Fort-William we booked by the coach for
Inverness, and, having breakfasted in a leisurely

way, we strolled to take possession of the box seats, which we had made a point of securing, when, lo,! we found ourselves forestalled by no less a personage than the redoubted Dr. Candlish, and with him Dr. Beith of Stirling. Of course we remonstrated against the *intrusion*, but at first to no purpose, and it was only on appealing to the civil powers (in the coach-office) that we were restored to our status. 'Sorry to *depose* you,' said our friend to Dr. Candlish, as he unwillingly dismounted. But I am happy to say that the affair passed off good-humouredly, and with no worse results to the two reverend Free doctors than their being relegated to the dignity of a post-chaise to themselves."

So writes Mr. Smith of *Fintry* — flippantly enough, as I may be pardoned for saying. Dr. Lee did demand, for himself and his friend, the seats which he had, as he said, the previous evening paid for. I answered that they had been paid for by us at an earlier hour. We sat still. I begged Dr. Candlish to be firm. The proprietor mounted the coach, and addressed himself to me. It was not to claim a right he did so, not to charge us with *intrusion*, but to prefer a very humble petition. The engagement of the seats by me, which he admitted, had been of so long standing

that the clerk at the coach-office had overlooked
the fact of their having been given to me, and had,
by mistake, let them last evening to Dr. Lee. I
said that mattered not : we could not yield to
Dr. Lee. In fulfilment of what I had pledged
myself to do, I now offered the full fare to *Inverness,* for we could not yield the seats ; our pre-
arrangements for the day's journey were such that
we could not. He begged, as a particular personal
favour, that we should give up the seats, and
engaged to put a chaise and pair at our disposal,
for ourselves, to carry us to Invergarry Inn, without a moment's delay. I saw my fellow-traveller
begin to waver. I begged of him not to give way,
for he could not foresee, as I foresaw, what must
be the consequence if he did. For a moment I
thought I had succeeded. But I was mistaken.
Dr. Lee addressed to us some gibing words, and
waited, in an attitude and with an air not pleasing
to me, for our coming down, as if we were bound to
do so admitted of no question. This made me all
the more determined. Dr. Candlish, however,
made an end of the discussion, first by throwing
down his plaid, and then, with his usual alacrity
and good humour, by generously following the
plaid and recovering it. What could I do but follow ? I did so, not, I confess, in very good temper,

Judging between the Edinburgh doctors, whilst not overpleased with either, I certainly admired the one considerably, at the expense of the other. A few words addressed to Dr. Lee, to explain the difficulty which he created for us, seemed only to amuse him. A moment sufficed for removing our traps from the "boot." The coach was off. We were left behind, looking, as I thought, not a little foolish.

Certain disappointed-looking personages attracted my notice, who appeared to be "hanging on," to whom I suspected the chaise had been promised as it had been to us. They were coarse-looking country people of the drover class, and such as drovers have for followers. My suspicion proved to be well founded. The chaise drew up. I observed them approach it.

"Now," I said to Dr. Candlish, "do follow me, and do as I do this time; it is our only chance."

"I will," was the resolute answer.

I hastened to the door of the conveyance; got it into my hand, held it, beckoned to my friend to hasten his steps, turned my back on the intruding party, quietly resisted their attempt to possess themselves of the carriage, and felt confident of success. I had reckoned without my host. They rushed to the opposite side, opened the door there, and began to occupy the seats. I at once stepped in, endeavoured to hold two seats, but endeavoured to do so in vain. I took one, however, and succeeded in getting my amazed travelling companion fairly within the door. He had witnessed the scene with great composure, and, as I imagined, in a somewhat frolicsome humour. I could have preferred to do the same ; but what was to happen with regard to our appointments and engagements for days to come? Or how were we to keep promise with the many, along the whole line of our projected ' route, who expected us? The conveyance was crammed with large, tobacco-whisky-smelling, greasy, vulgar fellows. I expostulated in "both languages," told them our position of difficulty and our prospects. I pleaded the promise of the coach proprietor that the chaise should be entirely for *us*. The proprietor was nowhere. He had disappeared conveniently for the intruders. They took it all coolly. They were in possession. That settled the question. I might spare my pleading.

A one-horse vehicle made its appearance in the distance, obviously to supplement the chaise. The horse looked a done animal, not fit for almost any work.

"Ye had better tak that," one of the inmates of

the chaise said to us ; "that maun be the ane for you."

We declined to act upon this suggestion, and chose to accept our unhappy position as we were. So the matter ended. There were five of us within, and one with the driver outside. Dr. Candlish and I alternated sitting and standing during the whole journey. In this he had the advantage of me, because of his stature—that being less a good deal than mine, and not requiring so much stooping when he stood. We were in LOCHABER, and among "the Cameron men !"

I had sent a message by the coachman of the Inverness *stage* to. the *Invergarry* innkeeper, to inform him that we were on the road, and to request that his conveyance should be kept for us. I had not much confidence that this functionary would prove more faithful than his employer. If other parties, his passengers, desired to have the Invergarry gig, he could, I was persuaded, easily be induced to hold his tongue. . So it proved. When, two hours after time, we arrived at Invergarry Inn, we found that, despairing of our coming, the "machine" had been let to others who had come by the coach, and was now away on an excursion in the direction of *Invermorrison*.

I had made up my mind to this. I had expected it, and was not overmuch chagrined. But what was to be done? Mackay, the innkeeper, was annoyed, and sincerely sympathised with us. We could ascribe no blame to him. He was willing to do everything to oblige us. He had a CART. He could nail a plank across, and so make a seat for us. His only horse, beside the one which was away, was "in the hill." "It might take some time to find him." I too well knew what a *wide* word being "in the hill" was. An hour might suffice to discover, and to apprehend, the wanted quadruped, two might be required; or a whole day might be consumed in the enterprise. But what could we do? Scouts were dispatched to scour the hill.

" Have you seen the horse lately?"

"In the morning early he was seen, but not since."

" Can he be very far off?"

" That we cannot tell."

Dr. Candlish seemed amused and interested. Throughout our journey from *Fort-William* he was gay, courteous, and became even fascinating, as it seemed to me, to our unwashed fellow-travellers. He saw that a *crisis* had occurred in our circumstances at the *Invergarry* Inn. It seemed rather to produce a pleasant excitement in his mind, and he showed himself equal to the occasion.

Early dinner was ordered. The cart was got out and washed. The plank was provided, and securely fastened on both sides, over the axletree. There was no support for the back. We all gave our aid in preparing this improvised carriage, Dr. Candlish being, certainly, not the least active of us. It was to be our means of transport for a journey of *ten* miles to *Tomandoun*—a good road, though uphill. We might be compelled to use it for *nine* miles more, to *Cluny* inn, to reach which we should require to traverse one of the highest mountain roads in Scotland. Nay, perhaps we might be compelled to use it as our conveyance for *twelve* miles beyond *Cluny*, on to *Shielhouse*. But what could we do? Dr. Candlish was gay as a lark. I had recovered my equanimity. The weather was fine. I foresaw that we were in for an adventure, and this did not distress me.

The want of a night's rest occasioned neither to my friend nor me, in prospect, much discomposure. I anticipated with interest calling his attention, at various points, to the beauty of the scenery along the line by which we had to pass, and the pleasure of listening to his observations thereon.

We dined comfortably, and felt quite equal, as we thought, to the labours which lay before us.

Two hours had sufficed for *finding* the horse.   In that space the "hill" had been successfully searched.   By the time he was yoked in our extemporised carriage, the sun had begun to decline towards the west.   Three o'clock, or a little more, saw us in possession of seats, from which we had no fear of being dislodged by any pretentious doctor ; and, after a hearty farewell to our kind host, we jogged on.

I shall not occupy time in describing the banks of . *Lochgarry*, or the charming moorland sweep into which we advanced, after leaving behind the weeping birches and the romantic accompaniments of that sweet inland lake.

We made our first stage in wonderfully good time.   At *Tomandoun*, to our delight, we found a shaky, four-wheeled, tumble-down vehicle, in which we resolved to trust ourselves, at least for one stage, it might be for two.   Our new carriage had springs—such as they were—decidedly the worse for wear, but still we believed strong enough for our weight.   They once had been springs. The sides and the floor of this worn-out thing were very dilapidated, yet it offered, upon the whole, a fair prospect of holding together for our time.   We were selfish enough not to care much for its future. With a fresh, at least with a new, horse, we proceeded to encounter the formidable ascent from *Tomandoun* on to *Cluny*. The ascent, as every-one who has traversed it knows, is, on the side from which we advanced, very long and very dreary. The night was approaching; our horse-power was weak; whilst our equipage was neither promising nor imposing. Yet we went on. The lad who drove us was respectful and attentive, willing to save his horse by himself walking when he considered it necessary, which he did more frequently than we approved of. Night fell on us ere we reached the summit. We began to feel heavy. It had been a long day to us.

"I once had an adventure here," I said to my companion. "If you like I will narrate it. The story, though of no great interest, may occupy us as we go on our way, now that scenery can no longer engage us; and it will show what risks Highland ministers sometimes encounter when in discharge of duty."

" Come away; let us hear it. Be sure that it is not a ghost story."

" Not *that*," I said; "nothing having its seat in the imagination, but a reality—a true story, and no mistake."

" Go on, then."

" It was in the month of February 1835. I had

been in the south, and was on my return home to Glenelg by the road which we are now travelling. From some derangement of the steamboats—a matter of common occurrence in those days— whereas I ought to have been landed at the *Inver-garry* Locks on the afternoon of the Friday in time to reach the inn at *Invergarry* that evening, I was not landed there until the Saturday forenoon. My dogcart had come on Friday evening, my purpose having been to proceed early on Saturday morning, that I might get to my manse that day in good time for being in my place for the Sabbath's work on the morrow. As it was, the afternoon instead of the morning saw us on our way. My outfit was different from that with which we are now con- tenting ourselves. It was a light vehicle. The animal yoked in it was a fine mare reared on my glebe, young and sprightly. My servant was a boy of courage, though not of much experience. When we reached *Tomandoun*—the halting-place which we have just left behind—we had still some little daylight. Our pace, in travelling from *Invergarry*, had been more rapid than it has been to-day. At *Tomandoun* a sprinkling of snow lay on the ground—not more than an inch in depth. We could see, as you may judge, but a short way before us along the road by which we were to travel. The people had told me that I might expect to find the snow deeper as I proceeded towards the summit, and that there it might prove to be of a formidable depth. They advised that I should not attempt to cross the mountain. As it was a matter of much importance that I should get home in view of the Sabbath, notwithstanding the suspicion thus expressed, I resolved to proceed. The warning which I had received proved to be too true. For a mile or two there was no depth of snow to hinder us, more than to forbid rapidity in our progress. The distant ridges, as they opened to our view, did look very white—too white to be accounted for by a partial fall. Besides this, we seemed to be getting into a region where the storm was in progress, as, we came to the conclusion, it had been all day. We persisted, however, though matters looked worse every step of our advance. Once it came into my mind that, I should retrace my steps to our last resting-place ; but we had come so far that I banished the suggestion and pressed on. Before we got to the summit, which you will see by-and-by, the snow was, at least, two feet deep on every part of the road. It had not yet begun to drift. That I looked upon as a mercy. There were no wreaths, which, had they existed, would have effectually

E

forbidden advance.   The smooth, unwrinkled, undisturbed, snowy winding-sheet enwrapped the entire landscape.   The outline of the road soon ceased to be discernible ; and we knew that we were, every moment, in danger of deviating from the path ; going over some one of the many low bridges which, as you may see, cross the mountain streams everywhere on this road, often at sharp angles ; or of getting into some bog, where our case might become desperate enough.   When we arrived at the summit, after much toil and much time, the wind rose and drove the snow directly in our faces.   This added immensely to our difficulties.   When we were about a third of the way to the summit, the boy and I had got out of the carriage and walked, divesting ourselves of as much of our outer clothing as we safely could. With all this the walk was exhausting in the extreme.   Having fastened the reins so that they should not drag, we betook ourselves to the rear, leaving poor *Rosa* (the mare's name) to find her way through the drift.   In this way we had the advantage of some slight shelter from the pelting blast.   We had the advantage, too, of planting our steps in the footprints of the noble animal—the boy coming in my wake, *Rosa* being allowed to lead.   She sank very deep ; but, I was thankful to observe, the wheels of our carriage did not sink; so that horse and carriage came to hold a somewhat awkward relation to each other. I hoped that, if we could get to the opposite side of the mountain, the decline being so great, we should advance more rapidly and more at our ease. I was satisfied that to go forward was as hopeful a course, now at any rate, as to attempt to return. I confess I did begin to feel that our position was not pleasant. We were wet up to the waist. I felt as if my face were being skinned under the ceaseless sweep of the pitiless storm. We began to be benumbed—my companion especially. He seemed desirous we should stop, to sit down and rest. This symptom alarmed me. We could make no more of headway than about sixty paces, when Rosa from time to time halted, and really required to halt, to draw breath. Thus our progress was disheartening, as well as slow. The stage, as you are aware, was but nine miles long; it was not yet half accomplished; and we had been contending with road and elements now for two hours. I at length formed the resolution of abandoning the conveyance, unharnessing the horse, taking up the boy behind, and riding on to *Cluny*, the next stage, which you will reach by-and-by. This, I began to fear, was necessary, if we were to escape with life. We attempted to carry the project into effect ; but the harness was swollen with the wet ; our fingers were powerless ; we could not undo a single buckle ; and when we had recourse to our knives to cut the harness, we could not make even a notch in any part of it. We were, therefore, shut up to proceed as we had been doing. Proceed we did.—toiling on in the fashion I have described. Perseverance, and the good hand of God upon us, carried us through. As I had hoped, when at last we began to go down hill our toil greatly abated. Moreover, the snow became less deep on the road, and, ere we had descended on *Cluny*, it had almost disappeared. On looking back, we could see the top of the mountain still enveloped in the cloud through which we had passed, and the snow accumulating there as it had been doing for a day or two. At *Cluny* everything was most wretched—no fire— no food—no refreshment of any kind. A few oats were procured, though with difficulty, for Rosa. Though I had all but made up my mind that we should be compelled to remain here, I saw, though the night had fallen on us, that we must needs press forward. Our road was all down hill. We had got, as we hoped, out of the region of deep snow ; so forward we went. My hope was realised. Little snow lay on this portion of the road, and through the Cimmerian pass which lies before us ere we reach this day's journey's end —*Scour Ouran* towering above — we arrived at *Shielhouse*, our present expected haven, late at night. Next morning (Sabbath) I was on the road by five o'clock. Snow had fallen during the night; and MAAM RATAGAN—of which we shall have some experience, as I hope, to-morrow— looked as if it were as highly favoured with this commodity as the mountain which had been our previous day's acquaintance. The experience then acquired gave me confidence. I calculated on giving *five* hours to the journey to Glenelg—one of only *nine* miles. I was going home. The Sabbath day's service awaited me, for I had no substitute; and I looked forward with comfort to the rest I should enjoy when my labour for the day was completed. It increased our confidence, that a few travellers—labourers returning from the south —pedestrians, who were waiting for some one adventurous enough 'to take the hill,' joined us. It was something that we were not to be so solitary as we had been on the previous day; and it was something, besides, that we had the beginning, and not the close of the day, for our work. I occupied my conveyance, with the boy, only for about a mile and a half. Immediately above the farm-house of Ratagan—which you will see to-morrow morning—the snow became so deep that we were compelled to alight and adopt the practice of the preceding day. The depth of the snow became greater as we advanced ; it was deeper than that which we had encountered on the other mountain. I found, however, that mare and vehicle sank only a certain depth, and that the snow was in such a condition that the former found footing sufficient to enable her to scramble onwards. All on foot kept in the rear, in regular line, not being able to give each other much help. You will see, when you come on the road, that at some points it is so steep that, without any obstruction to cause additional labour, it must be very hard work for any conveyance to make progress. Rest at fre-quently-occurring intervals is required even then of the man who is 'merciful to his beast.' In the state of matters with us this morning, you may judge what it must have been. In some places every advance of twelve paces required a halt, and then four or five minutes' space for recovering breath. At this rate we were compelled to pro-ceed. Having so much time to bestow on the effort, we looked confidently forward to a happy close of the toil. At the summit of the MAAM the snow was deepest, but the road there being comparatively level, our exertion to advance did not require to be so great. When we got fairly beyond the summit, and particularly when we came to face direct to the south and west, the snow rapidly grew shallow. As we descended the beautiful slope of the mountain, into the glen, it disappeared altogether. An hour from the summit brought me to my home. Having breakfasted and changed my dress, I repaired, with all my household, to church—a mile and a half from the manse —preached twice, and got back after all was past, a very wearied, but a very thankful, and to be a much-made-of and much-cared-for man."

Dark night had overtaken us by the time my story was finished. Some of the dangerous points to which I had referred were visible, scarcely visible, through the haze. Dr. Candlish satisfied me that he was interested in my narrative by the questions for additional information which he put to me in passing these as we went along.

When we arrived at *Cluny* it was bed-time. Some of the inmates of the so-called hostelry had retired to rest; and gladly should we have done so too had circumstances permitted. Two things forbade this indulgence. We learned, at once, that there was no "entertainment" either "for man or horse ;" and, had there been, we could not, thanks to Dr. Lee, have taken advantage of it. Another stage, and that a long one, required to be travelled, that we might keep time, and meet our pre-arranged engagements.

With scarcely any delay, and scarcely any refreshment for man or beast, we proceeded on our way. The road was downhill, a circumstance on which we congratulated ourselves. Moreover, though the night was dark, the weather overhead was fair. No stars appeared, and though they had, the horizon was too limited for our seeing many of them. Those who have travelled in the dark the road along which we were now advancing, know how deep the darkness is made by the shadow of the stupendous mountains which enclose it ; SCOUR OURAN, the mighty monarch of the vast wild, crowning them all. The defile, as may be conceived, is narrow ; and, though the path is guarded by low parapet-walls, we were often close enough to precipices, at various points, to create for us one of the elements of the sublime, so that we "held our breath for a time," and "held our peace," as our general experience.

It was long past midnight when we arrived at SHIELHOUSE Inn, in the district of *Kintail*, and not far from the head of *Loch Duich*. Very thankful I was when we drew, or rather crept, up to the poor-looking hostelry. The silence which reigned in and around it attracted our attention, and somewhat startled us. Not a sound of any kind could we hear, unless it was, amidst the deep silence, the occasional feeble, responsive bleatings of sheep and lambs on the far off hillsides. Not a dog even barked or moved his tongue. What could it mean? We expected that the sound of our approach would have caused some movement. There was none. Our driver rapped at the door. There was no response. He rapped again, with the same result. No sound was heard. I got down, and betook me to the door; knocked; shook it; tried to force it open; yet there was no sound, and no prospect of our getting admission. The house seemed to be under the power of enchantment, such as the *Arabian Nights* describe. What could it mean? Had the house been vacated? Had the inmates deserted it? We repeated our efforts to get admission, but no one answered. It was tantalising,—in our circumstances it was provoking. Something, however, must needs be done.

I knew the house well. I knew where the kitchen window was to be found. If matters

were as they were wont to be, I was sure the
window was not fastened. I could enter by it
and undo the bolts of the main door, admit my
fellow-traveller, and, if there were living beings
within to awaken, we could together rouse them.
I communicated my purpose to Dr. Candlish. I
cannot say he approved ; his opposition to my
proposal was not, however, so strong as to forbid
my putting it into execution. I found the
window at the back, as I expected, unguarded ;
and, having opened it, I easily introduced myself
into the large kitchen room, which was not un-
familiar to me. A minute sufficed to unbolt the
main door in front, and to admit into the interior
the minister of St. George's.

I must describe his appearance at this juncture,
only premising that, though the time of our deten-
tion had been long, even yet, up till this moment,
no responsive sound had been heard throughout
the dwelling invaded by us, if I except a single
deep anxious sigh which came from the "box-
bed," sunk in the wall, directly opposite to the
fireplace—at the distance of some twelve feet—a
sigh which died away almost immediately, and
passed into heavy breathing — the breathing of
soundest sleep. Well, Dr. Candlish was dressed
in a thick short overcoat, buttoned up to his chin.

On his head he wore a fur cap, a brown shaggy fur cap, with laps which came down over his ears, and left little more than the front of his face in view, save the spectacles which covered his eyes, the nose on which they rested, and the lips underneath, which were not motionless. My first step had been to look to the fire. I found in the place where I knew the fire usually stood on the floor (for there was no grate), a few peat embers. I gathered them together on the hearth, and, feeling for some fresh fuel, succeeded in getting hold of a few more peats in the neighbourhood of the hearth. A pair of bellows, too, not remarkable for their power as it proved, rewarded my search, and I entered on the attempt to revive the fire. This duty was abruptly taken out of my hands. " Give me that," Dr. Candlish said, seizing the instrument which I was using with the best of my skill. He drew under him a low stool which the partial light I had created revealed, sat down close to the ingle, and began to employ the asthmatic bellows with considerable vigour. The peats soon gave forth a stronger, though still a faint glimmer of light, which fell full on the face of the active operator ; especially on the spectacles, which fitfully flashed it back again. I stood in the shadow, and, to an eye outside, I must have looked a formidable object as the gleams from the hearth now and again illuminated my person. I do not describe my appearance at the time. The scene presented itself to me as extremely ludicrous. Had the grandees of St. George's, or had the listening throngs of admiring hearers, anywhere, of the hero of my story, set their eyes upon him at that moment! I could not resist a loud hearty laugh, which made the apartment ring again.

"What do you mean?"

My answer was a second laugh. But this was not all. A rustling in the bed in the wall, at this moment, drew my attention to that quarter. I still stood in the shadow, and the only visible object in the kitchen was the bellows-blower, sedulously occupied, with the most earnest expression, in producing light and heat, under the circumstances I have described. Opposite to him in the distance, the face of a young woman presented itself at the half open sliding door of the "box-bed." I observed her direct a glance at the fireplace. Her look (I saw it but for an instant) betokened the extreme of consternation. What her conclusion was I know not. But the exclamation which she uttered in Gaelic, as she hurriedly drew back and buried herself, head and all, under the bed-clothes, convinced me that she thought of my friend what she had no right to think. My laughter was renewed, and became quite uproarious. When I had explained, Dr. Candlish joined heartily in it. What the inmates of the "box-bed" (for there were three of them) thought and felt at that moment I cannot tell. Not to keep them in suspense, I went to the bed-side, spoke in Gaelic, gave my name, with the name of my fellow-traveller, and made them, as courteously as I could, to understand the predicament in which we were. They were satisfied, and, after a very short interval, the girl who had first shown herself, and one of her companions, having, within their dormitory, out of sight of us, dressed themselves sufficiently for the nonce, stood on the floor, prepared to serve us.

The secret of the unaccountable silence which prevailed on our arrival was easily told. They had had a "gathering" for "speaning the lambs."* For two nights in succession, they all—men, women, and dogs—had been out of bed, watching the lambs. This was the third night. The lambs had settled at last, and the watchers had got to bed. They were in their first sleep when we arrived; and no wonder that it was difficult to awake them. We had found it next to impossible.

* Separating them from their dams.

Glad, however, were we, now that success had so far crowned our efforts — efforts made in the fashion here set forth.

A wonderfully short time sufficed for preparing (we had not come altogether unexpected) a slight repast, and for "making down" the beds in the nice room *upstairs*, to which we were shown, and which was to serve for parlour, sleeping-apartment, and all. The beds stood one on each side of the entrance-door, directly opposite to each other. The window of the apartment stood directly opposite the door. Two o'clock — after our much-needed repast was done, and after we had given hearty thanks for the mercies of the day—saw us at rest. It was the first time, but not the last, during our tour, that we had slept in the same bedroom.

Arrangements were made for starting again at *five*. It was absolutely necessary we should do so. A fresh horse and conveyance were to be ready for us then. I feared we might oversleep ourselves, but our attendant servant-girl assured us that, as the "lads" had to be up with the first dawn of day to see after the lambs, and as then we should have noise enough of men and of dogs, there was little risk of our being left to untimeous slumber. She engaged, besides, to call us half-an-hour before *five*. We should thus have two hours and a half for repose. We hastened to bed. Instantly that Dr. Candlish laid his head on the pillow, I heard, on the opposite side of the room, the free breathing that betokened healthy, refreshing slumber. I followed suit, saying—

" So he giveth his beloved sleep."

Punctual to our engagement, we were on the road again a little after *five*, a beautiful autumn morning. It is something to ascend MAAM RATAGAN, under any circumstances, for the first time. It was truly enchanting this morning. The mountains, as we looked back, and as we looked to the north and south, were clear, sunlit, from their summits downwards ; fleecy clouds rested on their deep bosoms ; lights and shadows were never so strikingly contrasted. *Loch Duich* lay, far below, like a vast sheet of plate-glass, dark, motionless. All was stillness and apparent peace, SCOUR OURAN still the presiding monarch of the scene. Could human nature be as corrupt, desperately wicked, death-bearing, amidst such seclusion, such remoteness from the great world, as it proves itself to be amidst the seething masses and the haunts of gross vice in our great cities? Alas! I knew it could.

We went on gaily—now confident of arriving at Glenelg in good time to intercept the steamboat on her northern voyage, the object at which we had aimed. At the cost of much *extra*, and, but for the untoward event at *Fort-William*, unnecessary labour, we had overcome the difficulties which had seemed to forbid the accomplishment of the thing desired. What is pain when it is past? What is disappointment when we have survived it? We made good our object; and with that we resolved to be satisfied, forgetting the past. Down the long descent, by the delightful road from MAAM RATAGAN, past my old manse, beautiful for situation beyond all manses, we advanced to the Kirkton of Glenelg, which saw us enter its, to me, well-known single street, before eight o'clock. To the inquiry, "Is the BOAT in sight?" we had the answer, "No; she has not yet reached *Isle Oronsay*." This was enough. In an hour, not sooner, we might expect her arrival in the bay. Breakfast was prepared for us, and with excellent appetite and keen relish we partook of it.

As we passed into the open air a crowd of my old parishioners were assembled to see me, and to welcome my return to the glen. It was only my second visit since I had been removed from them in the autumn of 1839. The greeting was very cordial. The expressions of welcome and affectionate regard, on the part of the female portion of the assembled friends, were lively, and touched me not a little. The term of our ecclesiastical relations had had many things to make it memorable, and to awaken in their hearts and in mine recollections both pleasant and painful ; but, whether pleasant or painful, grateful to our feelings—recollections which we loved to recall and to dwell upon.

All were filled with joy to see my companion on this occasion. The name of CANDLISH was as familiar to them as a household word. He was a great man, they knew ; the leader of the Free Church ; the orator who swayed all minds in discussion and debate. They viewed him with intense interest ; but I saw a shade of disappointment (as I thought) on their countenances. The Highlanders of *Glenelg* and the neighbouring districts are not of the Celtic tribes—not of the same race as the Highlanders of *Islay* and *Argyle.* Of *Scandinavian* origin, their type of person is greatly superior to the other. They are tall, stalwart, ponderous men, with high features and a lofty bearing. Their women, in proportion, are the same. They are of the class of Highlanders who never think of a *great man* but as a man of gigantic stature ; who

F

do not care to realise the fact that a great soul can inhabit a body which is not in some due proportion to its greatness. They would have had my friend's " bodily presence " something different from what stood before them.

"'N-e so an duine mòr?" they said to me repeatedly in a sort of lowered tone. Had he exhibited the colossal proportions, specimens of which could easily have been furnished, for their gratification, from our Free Church ministers and elders, admiration would have been secured at first sight in its highest measure. If that was not the case at present, it did not interfere with the manifestation of their native politeness, or the expression of their respect and kindliness. When Dr. Candlish, in his affable, frank, joyous manner, spoke to them, they were greatly delighted. They speedily became impressed with his superiority, and gave me to know it by various exclamations in their own tongue, the meaning and force of which can be conveyed by no translation. His influence over them grew every moment, to my very sincere joy and satisfaction.

Our experience was the same all the way we travelled on our tour through *Skye, Ross-shire,* and *Inverness-shire,* to *Inverness.* In their admiration of my fellow-traveller, some of the Highlanders declared, and maintained, that they understood his *English* preaching, as well as the *Gaelic* preaching of their own ministers. I did not dispute with them this point, although I was willing to believe that the enthusiasm of the occasion might be excused if it produced some exaggeration.

By the time I had paid a visit to the church-yard, to the resting-place of my lamented children —four removed, within six short weeks, amidst circumstances elsewhere narrated by me,* the signal of the approach of the steamer was given.

The walk from the *Clachan* to the *boat-house*, from which point we were to embark, reminded me that the road along which we moved, as well as the boat-house, was the result of the people's industry in 1837, the year of famine. A considerable share of the provisions sent on that occasion in aid to the Highlands, fell to our parish. On my suggesting to the people that they might fairly *earn* their meal by doing work for it—work of a public kind—work which might be useful to themselves afterwards, instead of accepting the gratuity as a dole to *paupers*, they immediately consented, and the work then constructed remains till this day, a memorial of an independent and a manly feeling, which, at the time, greatly rejoiced me.

* " Narrative of successive Bereavements in a Minister's Family."

Many have since had the benefit of their industry; but the story is old, and there are few who remember, and few who know, aught about it.

We got comfortably on board our ship, our rowers in conveying us thither being not a little proud of their task. There we met, and were welcomed by, Dr. Begg, and with him Mr. Glass of Musselburgh, members of another deputation on the same errand with ourselves. I own I felt happy, my mind relieved, our object having been happily accomplished, when I stood on the deck at the appointed hour, with Dr. Candlish, all safe and sound—Dr. Lee notwithstanding.

Our destination, in the first instance, was *Lochalsh;* and there a temporary separation was to take place. As Dr. Candlish was advertised to preach next day (10th August) at *Portree,* he proceeded thither, not landing at *Lochalsh.* The other brethren landed and travelled to *Applecross,* where they had duty of a similar kind to discharge. As my work for next day was to recross the long ferry, through *Kylerea* to *Glenelg,* and to preach there, I remained at *Lochalsh,* the guest of the hospitable family at *Balmacara,* Mr. Lillingston and his amiable wife. It was my second visit, as I have said, since I had left the parish in 1839, then to become the minister of Stirling. By obtaining a grant from our building fund, and doubling the amount so secured by private subscription—a site having been kindly granted by the proprietor, Mr. Baillie—we had recently succeeded in erecting a Free Church in *Glenelg*. At the time of my present visit, though the fabric was by no means completed, it was sufficiently advanced to be occupied for a day. I accordingly preached there, in both Gaelic and English, to a crowded congregation, and so had the happiness to *open* the GLENELG Free Church. In the evening I returned to *Balmacara*, where further duty awaited me. In discharging it I was forcibly reminded of past times —times of much spiritual privilege and of deep interest to many. Thus ended our second week.

BEFORE I enter on the narrative of this week's progress, whilst I wait to be rejoined by Dr. Candlish, which will be early on the Monday, let me here record something of the remarkable man under whose roof we were to pass a little time, now and afterwards, before our present wanderings came to a close—a man whose memory will not soon be lost in the district of country in which, for many years, he was so prominent a character, and so highly and deservedly esteemed for his many virtues.

ISAAC WILLIAM LILLINGSTON, Esquire, of *Lochalsh, Ross-shire,* was an Englishman by birth. His father, Abraham Spooner Lillingston, whom, as eldest son, he succeeded, was proprietor of Elendon Hall, Warwick—a valuable domain in that county. His mother was the sister of the celebrated WILLIAM WILBERFORCE, the friend of the African, the enemy of slavery, and the eloquent advocate of evangelical truth and every good cause. The proprietor of *Lochalsh* was thus cousin-german of the late Bishop of Winchester, a man who, if he possessed his father's genius and eloquence, did not become of great name by walking in the same paths, or advancing the interests of religion on the same principles.

Mr. Lillingston was a Cambridge man. He had enjoyed all the educational advantages of the youth of the English aristocracy—advantages which prove so strong an attraction, perhaps so great a snare, to the youth of our Scottish gentry. That he had profited by the privileges which he had enjoyed, I think every one who knew him intimately would be ready to admit. That he set any high value on what scholarship had done for him, or that he sought to employ this for any high ends, according to the world's estimation, few would be ready to maintain. He was conscious of his power, and, at the same time, careless to use it, neither ambition nor vain-glory being the moving power within him.

He was an accomplished gentleman—graceful in his figure, tall, fair-haired, black-eyed, slightly made, of sweetest voice, but energetic, though calm and dignified in all his movements. It was said that he was unrivalled when he deigned to indulge in field sports. No one could come near him as a *shot*. The " wondering rustics " used to tell that they had seen him throw a shilling into the air, and, ere it reached the ground, shiver it with a bullet from his rifle. I never saw him perform that feat; but on one occasion I had an illustration of the confidence he had in the accuracy of his aim. We were proceeding together to take boat from the shore near *Balmacara* on a fishing excursion, his rifle over his arm. He had forgotten something, and ran back for it. I proceeded on my way. In a minute or two after, I heard his step hastening to rejoin me. At the same instant the report of his rifle startled me, it was so close, so sharp. My conclusion was that the piece had gone off by accident, and that some catastrophe, I could not for the moment tell whether to him or to me, had occurred. On looking to one side I saw, within two feet of me, a dog— shot dead. "Ah!" he said, "that dog has been of late worrying the sheep on the farm, and the shepherds have been urging me to have him killed. He was close to you when I observed him running along. I knew I could hit him without injuring you, except startling you. I hope I have not frightened you!"

Like many other Cambridge men, Mr. Lillingston was in the habit of coming to the Highlands for the vacation *reading*. Whether it was that he did his *reading* work easily, or that, having no professional end in prospect, he cared little about his tutor's authority and admonitions, at all events his excursions through the Highlands were many, and had speedily the effect of creating in him an inextinguishable admiration of the country, of its scenery, and of its population, in their manners, habits, pursuits, and peculiarities ; and, strange to say, their language, which ultimately he acquired. He seems, from his earliest introduction to the country, to have taken a lively interest in the moral and spiritual condition of the people ; and I have heard him say that, from the first, he felt impressed with the conviction that God's intention for him was that he should devote himself for life to the important purpose of serving the cause of religion in this wide and interesting field. That he did so, and that his efforts to do good and to communicate were greatly honoured of his Master—the Master whom he so faithfully served—all who knew his career can testify.

In one of his many wanderings through the Highlands, Mr. Lillingston became the guest, for a short visit, of Sir Hugh Innes, Bart., of *Lochalsh,* for many years M.P. for Ross-shire. There he met Miss Lindsay, the niece of Sir Hugh, and the heiress of his extensive estate. It was generally understood that Miss Lindsay's large fortune was invested in this landed security ;

and that, both for that reason, as well as her relationship to Sir Hugh (who had no family, never having been married), *Lochalsh* would certainly, one day, claim her as its possessor. That Miss Lindsay, though still very young, should have many to aspire to her hand, cannot be matter of surprise. One Highland Chieftain, especially, she might have had as her liege lord, to endow her with his wide-spread lands, and to dignify her lot with his famous title. She preferred the English wanderer, and, in due time, Miss Lindsay became Mrs. Lillingston. Thus she could then say, as she can still say, "I dwell among my own people."

Mr. Lillingston was an earnest student of the Bible. His library was very rich in theological literature. On his father's death, the English property was disposed of, and *Lochalsh* was made his family inheritance. Hither, his library, with other effects, was conveyed. The library was rich, particularly in the department of prophetical literature. Everything worth reading that had ever been published on the subject of prophecy was to be found on his shelves. Mr. Lillingston espoused, and very earnestly advocated and upheld, pre-millennial personal advent views. Perhaps, were he now among us, it might be alleged that he inclined also somewhat to the views of the Plymouth Brethren. However this may have been, his peculiarity of sentiment in either particnlar never interfered with his large-hearted catholicity, his spirit of most loving brotherhood for every man in whom he perceived love for Christ, ánd an honest desire to serve the spiritual interests of his fellow-men, seeking their eternal good. His entire time was devoted to the cause of human amelioration; and, believing that by the gospel, and by the gospel only—the gospel accepted and obeyed—such amelioration was to. be accomplished, he himself laboured, and secured others to labour, in the work of propagating its glorious truths to all whom he could reach.

He was passionately fond of yachting, and seemed to delight in daring marine exploits— much more so than many of his friends cared for —their alarms often affording him vast amusement. The ELIZABETH was famed on all the coast, from Cape Wrath to the Mull of Galloway. Her crew were select; and, when their master held the helm, every man required to be at his post, and to look out for squalls. In fine weather, any one might have the helm for him; not so when the sky darkened, and the white waves rolled.

The ELIZABETH was literally a missionary ship.

She was, by day and by night, at the service of ministers going to preach the gospel, and requiring the means of transit. No difficult questions were asked. If men professed to be on the "King's business," and if the cause was urgent on that account, the ELIZABETH's anchor was soon up, and her sails soon spread to the breeze. When the winds were denied, there was the huge sixteen-oared long-boat, which our friend always maintained could stand any sea that could rise, even in the Atlantic. I have had experience of this unique marine conveyance in bad enough weather.

Not merely as a passage boat, thus occupied, was the ELIZABETH famous all along the coast, but, above all, she was celebrated as a *Tract-distributor*. *Balmacara* looks directly to the entrance of the Strait of *Kylerea*. Vessels of all dimensions, from ironclads to the diminutive fishing smack, pass through this strait, especially in unsettled weather, to and from the Baltic and ports of the North, thereby avoiding the passage, always dangerous, on the outside of the Isle of Skye. In this Mr. Lillingston saw a wonderful opportunity of usefulness. He had religious tracts, the most worthy, in every language of Europe, provided in bales. Parcels of these were neatly made up, and so *loaded,* that, by the use of a little dexterity, they could be projected to a considerable distance. The men of the ELIZABETH were exercised thoroughly in the practice of throwing these projectiles. Their commission was to run their Yacht up alongside every passing ship and craft of whatever size, inquire politely, and in a kindly tone, "Of what country?" and, having been answered, immediately to cast aboard the parcel which the case, whatever it might be, demanded, and then to "bear away," to look out for some other object of interest of the same kind. Year after year this practice was pursued, not without very gratifying results, as was well known. The work was done in faith. Some might sneer. Many looked on and said nothing. The good man who had, in the warmth of his heart, originated this method of doing *his* Master's work, persevered in it, knowing whom he served, and what he honestly desired to accomplish.

His benevolence was unbounded.

" Is any sick ? the man of Ross relieves,
  Prescribes, attends, and med'cine makes and gives.
  Is there a variance ? enter but his door,
  Balked are the courts, and contest is no more :
  Despairing quacks with curses fled the place,
  And vile attorneys, now a useless race.—
  Behold what blessings wealth to life can lend !
  And see what comfort it affords our end !"

The Man of Ross.

At one time *Balmacara* House was literally converted into an hospital. The sick and the diseased, from every part of the country, without distinction, were received there. Dining-room, drawing-room, bedrooms—all were converted into wards for patients. The host and his lady confined themselves to one small parlour and one bedroom. The lawn in front of the house was covered with chairs and benches for the invalids, and the entire establishment of servants, household servants, and others, was made available for the business of nursing them and ministering to their infirmities. The presiding genius was Mr. Lillingston himself, who had a passion for administering medicine, his two great remedies being *mercury* and *Epsom salts*, these being aided by a vast variety of pills, either original or adopted. The thing lasted for a while. At length it began to be believed (at least suspicions became strong) that the hospital was not quite a safe one. Nobody, it was remarked, got better. Persons who had not much to complain of when they entered there got worse. Customers fell off. In the end there were to be found about *Balmacara*, as patients, only the knowing ones, who managed to persuade the good man (not a difficult task) that they were in poor health, and so succeeded in getting food, clothing, and money—accepted his medicines, at the same time, but took care not to swallow them—so *sorning* on him till even they became ashamed of doing so any longer. The eccentricities of *Balmacara* life disappeared when a young family began to bless the house. What was truly good never disappeared. Devoted earnestness in all that was holy continued. The friends of Jesus were ever received as if they possessed an indefeasible right to the hospitalities which were provided for them in the name of the Master. The voice of melody never ceased to be heard in the happy mansion. It cannot be denied that many who were not worthy took advantage of facilities which might have been better guarded by a wiser discrimination. But, in thousands of instances, the Lord Jesus was entertained in the persons of those who *were* worthy—who were his disciples indeed.

Mr. Lillingston believed with all his heart, as I have said, in the doctrine of the pre-millennial personal advent. His library was richly furnished with books, modern and ancient, dealing with this most interesting subject. To me he granted liberally the use of such books, dealing with the question, as I desired from him, by which generous conduct on his part I became considerably versed in the knowledge of what is advanced by the pre-millennialists, and with the arguments by which they sustain their views. In the very interesting study of prophecy (I speak of the study of prophecy generally), there are conclusions which seem to be well founded, and which may be true, that require, on the part of those who arrive at them, much faith and long-enduring patience, as well as willingness to suffer disappointment—at least for the time. This was eminently so in the experience of the proprietor of *Lochalsh*.

By his calculations he had made out, as other commentators of great name had done, that the year 1837 was to be distinguished by the fulfilment of prophecy in some great event. He did not conceal that *he* expected in that year the personal appearing of our Lord. He began to watch for it, especially during the night season, often depriving himself and depriving his household of natural rest. A remarkable natural phenomenon, which occurred towards the close of harvest in this year, greatly increased the excitement at *Balmacara*, and in all the region round about where the influence of *Balmacara* extended. An *aurora* of very unusual, perhaps of unprecedented, splendour occurred. Night after night, for nearly a week, when the atmosphere was free of clouds,

this wonder came into view. Never before had I
seen aught of the kind, so well defined, or so brilliant
and beautiful; and never since have I witnessed
anything to be compared with it. In the zenith—
right over head—there appeared a *corona*, a circular
open space, through which the clear sky was
visible, and there, far away, a single diminutive
star sparkled within the circle. From this centre,
itself of deep blue, there radiated in every direction, embracing the whole visible heavens, columns
of light, exhibiting every colour (as it seemed to
us), from deep purple to the palest yellow, including green, orange, and red. The wavy motion of
those alcoved columns produced a sublime effect.
It was impossible not to be awed by the sight. It
seemed so likely, too, that the circular open space
above us, was made there designed for some special
manifestation. That the visible horizon is limited
in a district so remarkable for high mountains as
Lochalsh, may account for the whole heavens being
occupied with those gorgeous *streamers*. In a
wider horizon their extent might have been cur-
tailed to the eye. To our apprehension, it seemed
as if within the range of the *corona* and its append-
ages was to be inaugurated, in the view of all
mankind, the great event which the friends at
Balmacara so earnestly looked for. But we were

G

mistaken. We waited in vain for some manifestation. None came. After a short period of expectancy on the part of those who were more or less affected by the phenomenon, the *streamers* disappeared. Human life in *Lochalsh* returned to its wonted course. Good Mr. Lillingston retained his convictions notwithstanding; pursued his researches; repeated his calculations to test their accuracy; and reverted to the assurance, which he had held so firmly, that, ere long, his conclusions would be seen to be according to truth. What had occurred did not by any means shake his faith in these.

"I was told of a poor peasant on the Welsh mountains, who, month after month, year after year, through a long period of declining life, was used every morning, as soon as he awoke, to open his casement window towards the east, and look out to see if Jesus was coming. He was no calculator, or he need not have looked so long; he was no student of prophecy, or he need not have looked at all; he was ready, or he would not have been in such haste; he was willing, or he would rather have looked another way; he loved, or it would not have been the first thought of the morning. His Master did not come, but a messenger did, to fetch the ready one home. The same preparation sufficed for both; the longing soul was satisfied with either."—*Fry*.

This was, as near as possible, the case with the proprietor of *Lochalsh*. The Lord called him home at a comparatively early age—when he was something above forty.

It will easily be credited that this amiable man was superstitious. His mind was eminently of that cast. He delighted in the marvellous, in superstitious religious anecdotes. Stored with these, somehow he was ever acquiring fresh accessions to his stock. Many of these stories, dealing as they did with the preternatural, were very exciting, though they were all intended, and perhaps, in some cases, were calculated, to lead the thoughts to the one Rock of confidence, and the one place of refuge in all dangers. Impressions were often made, which, painful and not quite profitable, one desired to shake off, but found abiding with him notwithstanding; the attempt to send them away by no means succeeding amidst the surrounding circumstances. In listening for a long winter's evening, amidst the dingy light of a large apartment, to such recitals, one felt as if breathing an infected atmosphere, and in spite of himself became enervated and unmanned, a prey to foolish imaginations and groundless fears.

I was on a visit, of a day or two, on one

occasion at *Balmacara* House. I had asked the use of some medical books from my kind friend, who was so ready, at all times, to furnish me with other books. His library was rich in literature bearing on the treatment of disease in every form. My children were, at the time, suffering under measles, and I desired to study, for their benefit, what related to that disease, especially to learn what means should be employed for its removal. I was informed, in reply to my application, that, whilst all other books might be borrowed from his library, medical books, by a stringent rule, could not be. But, if I came to the house, I might, if I could, read all that his library contained. I accepted the invitation. At home we were not within reach of professional advice and attendance ; I set myself, accordingly, to get possession of all the information I could from Mr. Lillingston's books, taking copious notes. At the close of this work, a long evening followed, which was passed in the way I have described above.

I retired to my bedroom before midnight. It was a large attic room at the east end of the house—an attic so large, that four beds were placed in it, one at each of the four corners. The door was directly opposite to the fireplace, which stood in the centre of the gable wall. The bed prepared for me, on the night in question, was to the left of the fireplace, the foot of the bed being towards the fire, which was shaded off, and out of sight, by the thick bed-curtain. The door was in full view of my bed, to the left. None of the other beds was occupied. No one slept that night in the main body of the house (the servants' apartments were in the two wings) except Mr. and Mrs. Lillingston, and myself. Their bedroom was situated on the ground-floor. The drawing-room floor intervened between it and the attic which I occupied.

I had gone to bed. After a little, I fell asleep, and I slept I know not how long. Suddenly I was awakened by what I imagined was a loud knock at my door. I opened my eyes: the fire was still burning, but was about to expire. I called " Come in." No sooner had I done so than I saw the door slowly open. A man of gigantic stature, of huge proportions, red-haired, half-dressed, his brawny arms bare high above the elbows, presented himself to my view. I saw him distinctly advance, not towards me, but direct to the fireplace, the glimmering light from the grate falling on his massive frame. He carried a large black chest, which appeared to me to be studded with brass nails, and to be so heavy as to tax to the utmost his strength, stalwart figure as he was. I saw him pass the foot of my bed, as if turning to the side of the fire next the bed towards the opposite angle of the room, on the same line. The black chest seemed to grow into a coffin of dread dimensions. In that form I saw it but for a moment. My bed-curtain almost instantly concealed from my eyes the bearer and his burden. He set it down with a crash which startled me, as I thought, and which seemed to shake the house, and, as I believed, fairly aroused me. I tried to look round to the fireplace, but I saw nothing. Everything was as I had left it on going into bed. The vision had passed. In whatever condition I had been previously, I felt confident I was, by that time, thoroughly awake. Reflecting on the incident, I soon set the whole affair down to a fit of nightmare, brought on, perhaps, by the conversation in which I had been so deeply interested before retiring to rest, and which had somewhat excited my nervous system. In a short time I had got over my agitation, and was composing myself to sleep, when I again suddenly heard a knock at my door. I raised myself on my elbow, with a resolution to be at the bottom of it, and said firmly, perhaps fiercely,

"Come in." The door opened,—when Mr. Lillingston appeared, in his dressing-gown, a light in his
hand. As he was in figure tall, though not robust,
and of a reddish complexion, his appearance
slightly resembled what I had previously seen.

"Have you been ill?"

"No; I am quite well."

"Have you been out of bed?"

"No; I certainly have not, since I lay down."

"Mrs. Lillingston and I have been disturbed by
hearing heavy steps in your room, as we thought,
and by the sound of the falling of some weighty
article on the floor."

"There must have been some mistake."

He bade me good-night, withdrew, and left me to
my reflections. Sleep came towards morning. At
breakfast, when we all met there, the noise which
had been heard became the subject of conversation.
I made no mention of the *vision; that* I kept to
myself. I suggested that something might have
fallen directly overhead in the drawing-room.
We went and examined it, but nothing could be
seen; all the furniture stood, every part of it, in
its wonted place. Had we been able to explain
the *noise* there would have been nothing in the
occurrence that might be accounted uncommon.
Even with that unexplained (the *giving*, or yielding,

of some joint in a piece of furniture might have
done it), there was nothing very unusual in what
had occurred. I would have forgotten it altogether,
but the succession of deaths in our family just a
year after—four children, as already noted, being
taken from us within a few weeks—brought up the
remembrance of what I had seen, and I felt a
strange—an unreasonable inclination I am willing
to admit—to connect the two things, and to conclude that what I had witnessed, or imagined I
had witnessed, in the *Balmacara* attic, was a kindly
presentiment or pre-intimation of sorrow to come.
It had some effect in making my heart, and another
heart too, tender, in anticipating trial which might
overtake us, for which we felt it became us to
stand prepared—trial of a kind that we had not, at
that time, ever tasted.

I only add that my affection for Mr. Lillingston
was strong. With eccentricity, to a certain extent,
the existence of which his warmest admirers would
not gainsay, he was a holy man, devoted to doing
good, never off his Master's work. In all the
region in which his property lay he exerted a
mighty influence of a most beneficial character.
His liberality and generosity to the poor became
proverbial. In one department it was eminently
so: I mean that of assisting promising young

men with pecuniary aid for pursuing their studies with a view to the ministry. There were friends who thought that in this, as well as in his charities generally, greater discrimination and a more diligent examination of the cases which claimed his patronage, would have been an advantage. He cared not to have such views presented to him. It could be no excuse, he would say, to withhold one's bounty, that the objects to whom it was extended were unworthy and ungrateful ; for God makes His sun to shine on the evil and the good, and His rain to fall on the just and the unjust : all are the objects of His bounty. Such was ISAAC WILLIAM LILLINGSTON. To him, that which the Christian poet wrote of another, might justly be applied :—

" Laurels may flourish round the conqueror's tomb,
  But happiest they who win the world to come ;
  Believers have a silent field to fight,
  And their exploits are veiled from human sight.
  They in some nook, where little known they dwell,
  Kneel, pray in faith, and rout the hosts of hell ;
  Eternal triumphs crown their toils divine,
  And all those triumphs, ——, now are thine."

Cowper.

II.

On the morning of Monday, 11th August, Dr. Candlish was expected to arrive at *Balmacara*

House, by steamer from *Portree.* Several friends, clerical and others, had come in the happy expectation of meeting him. The party was considerable. We had had breakfast ; but the table was spread afresh for the expected guest, whose appearance was longed for. It was a favourable opportunity for our hospitable entertainer to agitate his great question, the pre-millennial advent. An amicable, but animated discussion took place, in which we all joined—some taking the side of our host, and others opposing. His *exegesis* of a particular passage was questioned. The true meaning, however, it was admitted on all hands, must be decided by the power which belonged to a Greek particle occurring in the passage. As on this point we could not come to an understanding, it was resolved that the decision should be left to Dr. Candlish, and that we should all stand by his award, whatever it might be.

By-and-by the whistling sound of escaping steam is heard. The "BOAT" has arrived in the bay from *Portree.* Some of our party hasten to the shore to receive the passenger for whose arrival we have been longing. The *Balmacara* barge has gone off to receive him, and all are on the tip-toe of expectation. Mr. Lillingston has, meanwhile, retired to his study. Dr. Candlish enters, looking somewhat cold, and undoubtedly feeling hungry. He is welcomed very cordially by our warm-hearted hostess, and by all friends present. Breakfast arrangements are pressed on by footmen and servants running hither and thither. In midst of all Mr. Lillingston enters on the scene. He appears with his Bible under his arm—a notable Bible—a large octavo substantially bound—nothing ornamental —but its outer margin, in front and at both ends, written over in a most original way with the names of the respective books of the sacred record, a device by which the possessor of the Bible is able, with wonderful facility as well as wonderful rapidity, to turn to any of the books, and to find, without almost any delay, the particular chapter which he desires to quote from. I had prepared Dr. Candlish for some things which he might expect on coming to *Balmacara*. A hearty welcome is accorded by the head of the house to our distinguished friend—a welcome at least as hearty as any he had hitherto met with. But this is barely done, and he has certainly no more than taken his place at the table, and begun a breakfast which strongly solicits his appetite, than the question which had been in debate, is laid before him in a somewhat learned disquisition, and *his* view earnestly requested. There is an expression in his eye indicative of his being amused ; more, perhaps, of his being annoyed at the interference between him and the "good things" spread before him ; most of all, of suspicion that some joke is being perpetrated.   This is suggested to me by a glance which he casts towards me as I sit quietly at a little distance observing the scene.   He is not to be done.   This he makes palpable ; for, paying little heed, in the first instance, to the statement with which the subject has been introduced, he sets himself to satisfy the cravings of his hunger, evidently with much relish, and leaves to those of us who choose, to maintain the discussion.   He indicates, at the same time, sufficiently for the satisfaction of parties, that he is not inattentive to what has been going on.   When the right time comes he gives us the benefit of his convictions.   His decision is in favour of the views of our host.   I am thankful it is so, as we all are, for it makes an end of controversy for the day.   The victory is accepted in good taste and with kindly feeling.   There is no exultation ; and we pass a happy and profitable day.

We have to close the day with what has always been the practice here when a minister, or ministers, form part of the company in the house —religious service—not for the domestics only,

but for as many besides, from the whole neighbourhood, as may choose to attend: On the present
occasion the congregation is very large ; drawing-
room, dining-room, hall, stairs and staircase, to the
top, being packed full of hearers. The speaker is
stationed at a point in the hall, near the entrance-
door of the house, whence his voice may extend to
the entire audience, though his person can be seen
only by a portion of it. Dr. Candlish is the chief
speaker, though I take part of the service—" in
the other language." We all feel that we have
enjoyed a time of privilege, and none more than
our esteemed friend Mr. Lillingston. He has never
before heard the minister of St. George's. He is,
however, to hear him again before our tour has
come to a close.

III.

Next morning, Tuesday, 12th August, we took
ship for Skye. The point at which we were to
land was KNOCK, in the parish of *Sleat*, then the
residence of a much-valued friend, known to me,
as all his father's family were, for many years.
I mean Mr. Colin Elder.

It was a bright morning, with a fresh breeze
from the north. The wind being off the land, the
breeze to us on the *Lochalsh* shore seemed light.

I knew it would prove otherwise once we approached the entrance into *Kylerea* strait. Through that strait lay our course, past the bay of *Glenelg*, keeping to the right, and past *Isle-Oronsay*, into the Sound of *Sleat*. The ELIZABETH, with her skipper and crew, all tried men, was placed at our disposal for the run. Immediately on going on board, and on our fastenings being thrown loose, Dr. Candlish took the helm. The skipper exchanged looks with me. I had never seen my friend "at the helm," in the present sense, before; but I had full confidence that he would not have undertaken it unless he knew his competency. This much I managed to communicate to the man properly in command. The result proved the correctness of my conviction. The sail through the Kyle, with an ebb tide and fair wind, was exciting, for its rapidity. The tide must have been running at the rate of eight miles an hour; but though so much, the ELIZABETH outran the current sufficiently to keep good steering way. I thought the occasion was a novel one to the helmsman, especially when we got into the vortices caused at some points by the sweep of the sea; but he was quite equal to the duty then required at his hand. The skipper kept near; the men were each of them at his post. All went well.

" Merrily, merrily goes the bark,
　　On a breeze from the northward free ;
　So shoots through the morning sky the lark,
　　Or the swan through the summer sea."
Lord of the Isles.

We flew along the coast of *Skye*, leaving my old parish church at a distance to the left—on and on, past *Isle-Oronsay*, close on the right, until, about eight o'clock A.M., when our steersman put up helm, we ran into *Knock* Bay. There was no need to cast anchor. The ELIZABETH, now entirely in the hands of her commissioned master, "lay to" gracefully. The boat was lowered from the davits with great celerity, and we were comfortably landed on the shore. Our things were conveyed to the house by two of the yachtsmen, who soon rejoined their ship. Not long thereafter, we had the pleasure of seeing the ELIZABETH lying over to the coast of KNOYDART, on a long tack, by which she caught the "first of flood" sweeping back towards and through *Kylerea*, and was borne to her morning moorings, as we afterwards learned, almost as rapidly as she had conveyed us from them to our present haven.

The inmates of KNOCK House were scarcely out of bed. Our arrival, however, soon produced an altered state of things ; and we found ourselves

made cordially welcome to all that hospitality
which, in the Highlands, and very specially in
Skye, friends to whom we commit ourselves know
so well how to employ.

We had work on hand, for our visit was not
one of ceremony or polite formality. Weeks
before it had been arranged that we should, on
this day, preach here. Our place of worship was
a *barn* or *kiln*, supplied by our present host. By
noon the people of the district, to a considerable
number, had assembled, when we both preached,
of course in different tongues ; but in such manner,
in both cases, as to elicit the warmest expressions
of gratitude. As in all the localities which we
visited, there were here matters connected with our
Church which had to be definitely arranged, and
which were absolutely referred to our decision,
more particularly to that of Dr. Candlish. I never,
until this time, realised so vividly of what unspeakable benefit to the churches of primitive
times the visitations of the apostles must have
been. If stated regular calls, of a kind resembling
this of ours, by our leading men, not superseding
but aiding our presbyteries, were made to the out-
lying fields of the Church, the good accomplished
might be very great.

We were Mr. Elder's guests for the day. We

made his hospitable mansion our resting-place for the night too, and not a little enjoyed the intelligent converse of a man who, although living a most retired life, unknown to the world, was a thorough classical scholar, an *alumnus* of Marischal College, Aberdeen, and well read in all modern literature. One of his sons is the present minister of Woolwich, of the English Presbyterian Church. From Mr. Elder, Dr. Candlish received much valuable information as to the state of ecclesiastical matters in all the region where we at present were—information of which, as it may be well believed, he made good use when the time for doing so came.

Next day we were kindly conveyed across the country to ORDE, on the borders of Loch *Slapin*. The family at ORDE were not of our Church, but being old acquaintances of mine, I asked Dr. Candlish to accompany me to the house for a very short call, which he kindly did. The visit was counted an honour, and I received hearty thanks for having prompted it. From here we crossed the sea by boat to the *Strathaird* coast. We were in the close neighbourhood of the *Spar Cave* and *Coruisk*, but the work which we had on hand for the day forbade our availing ourselves of the

H

opportunity of visiting these wonderful natural phenomena.

A Free Church was about to be built on the moor, between the sea we had passed and *Strathaird* House, which stood farther on, and higher up on the face of the mountain. It was then possessed by Dr. M'Allister—he and his wife (who was from the neighbourhood of Stirling) being earnest and intelligent friends of our Church. Part of the preparations for proceeding with the erection of the place of worship referred to had been made, and we were expected, on the day of our visit, to hold some service in connection with the ceremony of laying the foundation-stone. The weather was cold, drizzly, uncomfortable; the place was bleak and without shelter. Yet it was an August day, and all the forecastings were in favour of the hope that "it would clear up." Towards afternoon it did, but not until our work was completed.

Following the usual order which we had agreed to adopt in our peregrinations, I began the services of the day in the language of the country, preaching in Gaelic. A large congregation had assembled. I had more than once in my experience been made to know the great disadvantage of preceding Dr. Candlish in any public meeting. . Even in the

Highlands I was made to feel this, arising from the naturally restless desire on the part of the assembled multitudes to hear my friend. That I spoke in the language which they best knew, and most loved, put me more on a par with my friend than if we had both spoken in the same tongue. Still, I felt at a disadvantage, and disliked to appear to be standing in the way of the gratification for which I could not but see the people were longing.

Dr. Candlish laid the foundation-stone—masonic honours being omitted—and afterwards delivered an address which charmed the Highlanders, and which they declared they quite comprehended. I never listened to anything more gratifying, for its clearness, and simplicity of expression. It was not a sermon, but an address on our great Church question. The Highlanders of that generation ('tis all but thirty years since) well understood why, and on what grounds, they had ceased to be of the Established Church, which they counted, and justly counted, to be no longer the " Church of their fathers." No art or sophistry could *then* have made them believe that the cause of the Disruption was anything else whatever, than the oppression to which the Church had been subjected, by the unconstitutional interference of the civil power with the inalienable spiritual liberties which she holds from Christ himself. That this interference touched the matter of the appointment of ministers, and other office-bearers, made the evil all the more manifest, all the more easily apprehended, and all the more sternly resented. In the times to which I am referring, there was nothing else to set forth as the great truth, the maintenance of which had led to our separate condition. No one dreamed of introducing any other topic in explanation of, or as accounting for, the change, or as that which equally had demanded our advocacy. Certainly Dr. Candlish believed that he was speaking to the whole question of our great Disruption testimony, when he expounded the principle of the spiritual liberty of the Christian people, and when he demonstrated by historical references, and from historical details, that deprivation of this liberty—under such compulsion as made it clear that, if we did not abandon our connection with the State, we must necessarily be guilty of great sin against our Lord and King— was the cause of our separation. That the address was chiefly historical, and that it spoke of events with which his hearers were more or less acquainted, made it all the more easily comprehended, and all the more gratifying. For my part I felt both refreshed and instructed, and volunteered, at the

close of the English, to make a short statement in
the Gaelic tongue, in supplement, to announce my
concurrence in all that had been said, and to translate some things which I believed some of them
had difficulty in exactly taking up. In this capacity of interpreter, I provided an index to Dr.
Candlish's speech, for which I received most cordial acknowledgments. Our meeting was a great
success.

The open-air work being ended, we adjourned
to Dr. M'Allister's house, where a comfortable
repast, most cheerfully bestowed, reinvigorated us
after our morning's exertions. We were all pleased,
and a strong feeling prevailed that the proceedings
would produce good and profitable results throughout the district. But our programme for this day
(13th) was not yet exhausted. The two travellers
had still something on hand to accomplish. Moreover, their time was running done, and, though
the season was still, according to usual phrase,
summer, we knew that moonless nights in August,
are often among the darkest nights in any of the
seasons of the year. We were not unwilling to
enjoy a little rest ; but,

> "Nae man can tether time or tide ;
> The hour has come when we maun ride."

We had engaged, by our arrangements made

weeks before, to meet Mr. Roderick M'Leod, minister at *Snizort,* at *Sligeachan* Inn, on the evening of this day. His part was to journey from *Snizort,* and to await us there. The following day had appointed for it, as its moiety of work, the visitation of *Bracadale* and *Dunvegan.* To arrive at *Sligeachan,* and so to fulfil our engagement, we required to traverse a trackless moor, upon which we were to enter a little to the left of Dr. M'Allister's house. The length of our prospective journey was some *eight* or *ten* miles. To walk such a distance over such ground as lay before us was out of the question. Dr. M'Allister knew this. He was too well acquainted with the necessities of travellers, who found out his hospitable abode in this region, not to be provided for such an exigency as ours was on the present occasion. He kindly furnished us with two small Highland shelties and a guide. Our traps were very light, for we had left our heavier *impedimenta* at *Balmacara,* and we felt no compunction in consigning them to the charge of our guide, who was to walk the distance we had to traverse on horseback, it being in his day's work to return with our cavalry to their accustomed pasturage.

The day had cleared up beautifully, and when, after a very grateful adieu to our kind friends at

Strathaird, we took horse, the sun shone with tempting warmth and brightness. We had, for the time, overlooked the fact that night falls much earlier in August, now nearly half done, than in June or the beginning of July. It never entered into our minds that we were to be benighted on the desolate moor which stretched out before us. The ride in ascending to the summit of the ridge was most interesting—every step of our progress revealing fresh beauties in the scenery. The *Cuchullin* hills rose gradually on our view as we advanced, until, when we stood on the highest peak of the range over which we were passing, those magnificent mountains stood before us in all their magnitude, *Coruisk* lying below imbedded in their bosom, and the widespread sea of the great Atlantic stretching away in all its vastness behind and beyond them. The prospect was grand beyond description—

" A scene so rude, so wild as this,
　　Yet so sublime in barrenness,
　　Ne'er did my wandering footsteps press,
　　　　Where'er I happ'd to roam.
　　The wildest glen, but this, can show
　　Some touch of Nature's genial glow ;
　　On high Benmore green mosses grow,
　　And heath-bells bud in deep Glencroe,
　　　　And copse on Cruachan-Ben ;

But here,—above, around, below,
   On mountain or in glen,
Nor tree, nor shrub, nor plant, nor flower,
Nor aught of vegetative power,
   The weary eye may ken."—*Lord of the Isles.*

It was impossible not to stand still and admire the glorious sun; the gorgeous reflection of his rays from the gently undulating great deep; the islands and islets which spotted the ocean here and there along the coast as far as our eye could reach; the dark, almost black, *Cuchullins*, on the left; the clear mountains opposite to the right, on which the orb of day was still shedding his light, as if favouring them, to despite their gloomy neighbours, all was entrancing. My companion was in ecstasies. The scene was worth undergoing toil to see. It was such a noble picture as Count Montalembert .labours to delineate. We stood, and stood, taking no note of time, until at length we bethought us that we might be preparing a difficulty for ourselves, for the sun was all but gone to rest under the western wave. On looking round, we saw that our guide had gone forward. "We shall surely overtake him," we thought. The ponies—we still holding in our hands the bridles—were contentedly cropping the grass, which seemed to them very sweet on the elevation where we stood. We mounted, and put them in motion. The rest had refreshed them ; it was a longer rest than we had intended, or than was wise in the circumstances, and they were not unwilling to proceed.

The descent was by no means easy. It was very precipitous ; the path was shingly—all loose rolling stones—and our ponies were shoeless ; their hoofs had never known the luxury of iron defences. One of the present riders, who had never before seen animals so dealt with, felt not altogether comfortable. The other, having had more experience in such matters, was, comparatively, at his ease on the subject. Without a slip or stumble, or anything approaching either, we got down to what certainly was more level ground ; but it was so low relatively to the mountains on each hand, as well as to those before and also behind us, that the nightfall, which had by this time come, brought, what appeared to us, impenetrable darkness. The sea, moreover, was no longer visible. The reflection from that vast mirror, had it been available, even though shadows rested on it, might have helped to alleviate the deep gloom which sank down on our path—our supposed path—for, verily, there was none to discern, even had circumstances permitted it to be discernible. No stars and no sky were visible overhead. All that we could distinguish was an uncertain clearness in the heavens; in the direction which we believed to be the *west*, towards which we were tending, nothing else was discernible. To be enclosed in such a mountain pass, the visible horizon being the smallest possible, must be something like being at the bottom of a coal-pit. To us it seemed to be so. We of course never got sight of our guide. He did not wait for our coming up to him, for probably he foresaw difficulties if he did. The ponies never stopped, never hesitated in their advance. I assured Dr. Candlish that they knew the way; that, if we could just ride them, carrying their heads with the bridles, not guiding and not attempting to guide them, only leaving them to take their course without interference, they would carry us, in their own time, to our place of destination. The path (if it existed) had evidently become too narrow for their travelling abreast. Assured that they knew which should be leader, I advised that we should leave the question of precedency to themselves. When we did so, I was gratified that the creature I bestrode led the way, so that, if we should encounter mishap, I should be the first to be involved in it. We resolved to take care that we should keep as close to each other

as we possibly could. We were able to inter-
change thoughts, and to keep up converse—which,
however, was neither theological nor metaphysical.
I was not sure that my friend had such confidence
in the poor brutes which carried us as I had; I did
my best to beget the confidence which I was sure
was merited.

The way began to appear very long. In such
circumstances we could not very well take count
of time. So far from being able to examine our
watches, we were happy when we caught view of
each other. We were evidently in for a Highland
adventure.

After a long while we came, suddenly, to a dead
stand. On examining into the cause, we found
ourselves abreast of a dyke—a drystone dyke—
more substantial, however, than a mere *rickle*, or
tumble-down gathering of loose stones.

"What say you to your much-praised ponies
now ?"

"I have lost no confidence in their sagacity
yet ; but let us do them justice. There may be
some opening, some wicket, through which we
may pass—let us see."

We rode along the wall to the right, and found
no such opening. We turned the ponies' heads
back by the way we had advanced, taking care that

we kept close to the wall. When we had groped our way back, the creatures stopped again, in as far as we could perceive, where they had stopped at first. We then urged them on, along the wall, to the left. The result was the same. On turning their heads again to the right, they advanced until they again came to a stand at the point, as we thought, where they had at first stood still.

"What are we to do?"

"It is not a case of much difficulty," I answered; "we must make a gate for ourselves."

"How?"

"Make an opening in the wall by throwing down a portion of it."

"I protest against that; it would be a breach of the law; it would be actionable; destroying fences, injuring property,"—and much more to the same effect.

"To break a *slap* in a stone dyke for a temporary purpose," I answered, "building it up again when we have served our purpose, will never, in the Highlands, be brought against any man as an actionable offence. Remember SHIELHOUSE. If I had yielded to you there, we should have been literally out in the cold till morning. If I yield now we shall fare worse than we could have done then."

He laughed, and said, "Have your own way, then."

" Hold my bridle ; let us keep the ponies carefully in hand amidst this darkness. If they go three feet from us we may not recover them."

It cost only a few minutes to make an opening in the wall at the point where we had been brought to a stand. There was no need to level the wall to the foundation, or even near to it. Moreover, it was no feat after all. The stones were evidently used to be treated as I was now treating them, so loosely did they rest on each other.

" Give me the bridle of my pony, and hold your own fast till I have completed my experiment, please."

The animal knew well what he was expected to do. Almost with the agility of a dog he leapt through the stile. His companion followed the example, both having perfect understanding of their duty. The minister of St. George's followed. At my request he held both bridles until I had built up the *slap*, and made the wall at least as good a fence against black cattle (for that was all it was intended for) as we had found it. We were once more in our saddles, leaving the healed breach behind us, *en route* for SLIGEACHAN Inn, the darkness, with every step in advance, growing, if possible, deeper.

Sometimes it seemed as if our ponies moved

along some beaten path, such was the sound their
bare hoofs produced ; more frequently as if they
trod the greensward besprinkled with heather.
We went quietly on, sometimes holding our
breath, endeavouring to catch any sounds which
might speak of speedy escape from darkness and
toil. More than once, but once particularly, we
perceived, from the sound of rushing water far
below us, that we were travelling along the margin
of some ravine, within which a stream, great or
small, pursued its course to the ocean. We inferred
that we were descending, however slowly, towards
the sea. Afterwards, we learned that the case was
so, and that we owed much to the sure-footed-
ness of the animals which carried us. It seemed
a very long night. No doubt we were miscalcu-
lating, and unnecessarily magnifying, its length.
At last a light broke on our view directly in front.
Could this be *Sligeachan ?* Whatever it might be,
our ponies kept plodding on in a direct line, as
we thought, towards it. Greatly did the light
distress us. It shone straight into our eyes, be-
wildered us, deprived us of the very partial power
of vision we had enjoyed, and made the darkness
all the more dark in our unhappy consciousness.
At length we came abreast of it, shining high up
on the sloping hill-side. Were our ponies to turn

towards it, or were they to leave it behind? The latter was their selection. They wheeled to the left, and, in a very short time, a shoulder of the mountain, or some rising ground that intervened, hid the light entirely from our view. It was a relief, of its kind, that we had passed it. We had thought that such a consummation was never to come, so protracted was its presence. That it did come proved progress on our part. We *were* advancing; there could be no doubt of it, though for so long a time the state of matters seemed to make that very questionable. It was possible we might be travelling in a circle.

We did not interfere with our steeds in their choice of our course, for more than one prudential reason, especially for the reason that we could distinctly hear, to the right, the brisk run of the stream along the margin of which we had been moving, and which lay between us and the house on the mountain's crest, from which the light had been shooting its rays at us. It would not have been comfortable to have had to ford a river, amidst the many uncertainties connected with such a feat in circumstances such as ours. From that I would have shrunk more than from breaking a *slap* in a dyke.—A quarter of an hour more of *dark* journeying.

" Don't you smell the sea ?"

" I do ; and I hear its welcome ripple on the shore, too."

Then, to our great joy, we saw light—not one, nor two, nor three, but a whole house ablaze with lights at many windows, directly in front of us, and evidently a stir of some kind existing, from the unceasing motions of the lights.

" There is *Sligeachan* at last ! Well done, ponies !"

" And thanks," we both exclaimed, " to the good providence of our gracious God." We were truly grateful and happy.

Considerable anxiety for our safety prevailed, we learned, at the inn. The guide had arrived early in the evening. He could not account for our non-arrival. Mr. RODERICK had arrived, expecting to see us before nightfall at our resting-place. With all his natural stolid equanimity, he had had certain uneasy apprehensions about us. We might be left in the open hills till return of day, and what would come of that? He had caused all the windows in the house in sight of the moor to be filled with lighted candles. This kind precaution had availed us for a mile—no more ; but he had done in that all *he* could do, and all that could be done, even although an accident had occurred, until the day returned. The guide, on being remonstrated with by us, coolly replied that the " beests kenned the way as weell as himsel—there was nae fear o' us if we let them alane." We gave instructions as to the " beests" being cared for, as well as their groom, and we saw no more of them ; for, long before we appeared, after the repose of the night, they had departed on their return to the hills of *Strathaird*.

We found our Snizort friend (Mr. Roderick M'Leod) in the *room* " upstairs," in which there blazed a noble fire. Right glad was the good man to see us—to see us in *Skye*, and to welcome us to his diocese. The table was spread with the tea apparatus, as well as with other articles than what the making of tea required, suggesting the not un-welcome thought that something more substantial than the beverage which cheers, but does not in-ebriate, was in preparation for us. There had been a great "take" of herrings in the loch. That morn-ing the fishermen had brought to shore herrings, in quantity and quality, such as they had not seen for years. The *quality* was soon put to the test by the party presently surrounding the table of the upstairs apartment of *Sligeachan* Hotel. Such *beauties*, and such a number of them, with all the appliances of the finest sweet butter, delicious cream, and other luxuries! How rapidly the herrings disappeared from the table, and in what numbers, it need not be told; neither need it be recounted who were chiefly distinguished in helping the disappearance. After some little discussion—renewed occasionally for a day or two—it was ultimately agreed to make this an open question, each of us holding his own view. Mr. Rory (a name by which Dr. Candlish delighted to call our friend, when he came to know that it was no *nickname*, but a contraction of the Gaelic *Ruaridh*), declined to be a judge in the matter. The assembling of the household for worship—for praise, prayer, and thanksgiving—brought the day to a close, and refreshing repose rewarded the toil and anxieties through which we had passed. The morrow had its labours in store for us—the same in kind as in the days past. The scene of these was to be along the coast from *Sligeachan* by *Bracadale* to *Dunvegan*. This I will make the next stage in our three weeks' tour; but ere we enter on it, and whilst we refresh ourselves in prospect of what we have yet to accomplish, a few pages must be devoted to the remarkable man who has met us at Sligeachan, and who is to be our companion for the remaining portion of our journey to INVERNESS, and to the meeting of the General Assembly there.

IV.

The story of Mr. RODERICK M'LEOD is not one simply of private interest. It is one rather of public notoriety. So, at least, it was in years which are gone, and to a generation which has all but passed away.

I introduce it here, not merely because Mr. Rory has joined us at Sligeachan, nor because the story affords an illustration of the state of matters in the Established Church in the North-Western Highlands at that period, but because I was in some respects connected with it officially, and can therefore speak to the facts from personal knowledge ; and chiefly, because the happy settlement of the question in which Mr. Rory was involved, and which, for many years, was the occasion of much anxiety to the friends of Evangelical religion, was mainly due to Dr. Candlish, who, above all men, has been singularly honoured in bringing to a happy issue many difficult and perplexing questions, threatening evil in our beloved Zion.

Mr. M'LEOD was cousin-german to the first Dr. Norman M'Leod, father of Dr. Norman M'Leod, Queen Victoria's favourite. Both were the sons of ministers of the Established Church, in the

Highlands. Mr. Rory's mother was the sister of Dr. Norman's father. Our friend inherited the natural talent—the genius—of the family, and, though he walked through life in a sphere more sequestered than that in which his more distinguished relatives moved, to those who knew him well he was in no respect inferior to either in intellectual endowments, whilst he was vastly superior to both in the higher qualities of the Christian life. It was his lot, notwithstanding, to be suspended by his Presbytery, from the office and work of the ministry, for a year or more; and like the oppressed Nonconformists in England, in the evil times of Charles II., he was compelled to withhold himself, except by stealth, from all work among his attached flock; ultimately, he was even subjected to a prosecution in the Church Courts, which contemplated deposition! This was the culminating point in a long series of proceedings which had their origin in motives, the nature and character of which I will now describe.

The allegation against him was, that he refused to dispense the sealing ordinances of our holy religion, Baptism and the Lord's Supper, in his parish of *Bracadale;* that he had caused a disregard of those ordinances to become widely spread in *Skye* and elsewhere; and that, through his

influence, that island and other districts of the
adjacent country had fallen into a condition of
great disorder and demoralisation. On the ground
of this alleged condition of things—all laid at the
door of Mr. Rory—his Presbytery felt themselves,
as they professed, called on, in the interests of the
Church, to proceed to the extreme measures to
which I have referred.

- The BRACADALE CASE had been frequently before
the General Assembly, and had undergone much
discussion there, chiefly on the technicalities, but
also sometimes on the merits. Through glimpses
thus obtained by the friends of religion, and the
leading ministers of the Evangelical party, a partial
knowledge of the real state of matters came to be
apprehended. The very solemn step contemplated
by the Presbytery of Skye in the case, arrested
attention, and brought our first men to the front,
to interfere in behalf of truth and charity. In Dr.
Hanna's "Life of Dr. Chalmers" a very interesting
account is given of the concern which this case
gave to that eminent friend of every good cause ;
of his communings with the first Sir Henry Mon-
creiff, and other leaders of the Evangelical party, on
the subject ; of his efforts (to his joy crowned with
success for the time) in behalf of the minister of
BRACADALE ; and of the arrest which, mainly

through Dr. Chalmers' interference, was placed on the threatened deposition. This was in 1827. Dr. Chalmers was in London when the Assembly met, and (as earnestly solicited by several friends) he came down to Edinburgh, expressly to use every means and all his influence for the preservation to the church of a man so worthy, notwithstanding his aberrations on the subject in question. After many earnest communings with him, Mr. M'Leod agreed to make the following declaration :—" With reference to the impression that the discussions concerning my conduct have produced as to my holding views and principles inconsistent with the laws and constitution of the Church of Scotland, I now declare my conviction that the same are agreeable to the will of God, and my entire willingness to obey them, and my decided resolution to adhere to them, without any mental reservation or qualification whatever ; and that, as I took no appeal, I acted wrong in disobeying the injunctions of the inferior court." On this declaration being laid before it, the General Assembly unanimously agreed " that the whole process relating to Mr. M'Leod is now at an end, and that there is no room for any further proceedings."

To show the sentiments which our best and ablest ·men entertained of the case, I give the following extract from the speech—a most successful one—which Dr. Chalmers delivered in the discussion before the Assembly, as one of the judges therein :—" In the history of this distressing case,". he said, "I do feel there is one ground of comfort, when I observe the Presbytery of Skye charging Mr. M'Leod with contumacy rather than with conscientious scruples. Now, in as far as that part of the charge is concerned, he is certainly on higher vantage ground than at the time when the libel of the Presbytery was drawn up. He has submitted to the views of the Presbytery on the matter of his suspension ; he has given up his own will to that of his immediate superiors ; he defers—and I am not sure that he is right in doing so—to the interpretation which his colleagues have given of the Assembly's sentence, as if it were still in force against him. But I enter no further into this, than to notice the subsequent conduct of Mr. M'Leod, as being the indication of the very reverse of contumacy. At a heavy expense to his own feelings, he has abstained from the duties of the pastoral office, and now stands before the Assembly in an attitude, to say the least of it, more fitted to conciliate his judges, than he did before the Presbytery at the time when the charges of the libel were constructed against him.

"Having said this much of the alleged contumacy, I feel less difficulty in characterising the difficulties of Mr. M'Leod on the subject of baptism, as partaking, to a certain degree, of the nature of scruples or scrupulosities; the difficulties, I am persuaded, of a thoroughly honest, but somewhat withal of an unenlightened conscience—of a conscience tender and sensitive and fearful, yet requiring the guidance of minds that have more of Christian experience, without, at the same time, having less of Christian principle and devotedness than his own.

"I can in no way go in with the barbarities which have been uttered against the gentleman whose case is at your bar.   He is not the oppressor of his flock; he is their conscientious overseer. It is not in a domineering spirit that he withholds from any one of them the privilege of the Christian ordinances; it is in the spirit of a right and religious tenderness—right, I mean, as to the feeling and general principle of it, whether right or wrong in its special application.   Even though wrong, this does not preclude him from the affection due to a brother, and from the veneration due to a man of his sensitive and spiritual delicacies. I might differ from him in judgment, and yet could not find·in my heart to have aught of the spirit of an adversary towards him; and I do think that scruples and sensibilities such as his ought to be dealt with in the spirit, and spoken to in the accents, of gentleness.. This is not a case for tyranny or for terror; it is a case for deepest sympathy. This is not an occasion on which to raise the tomahawk that strength or power has put into our hands, and brandish it aloft in brutal and barbaric triumph over the trembling victim who is beneath us. There is nought more revolting in cruelty than the skill and subtlety of its ingenious refinements; and never is the exhibition of it more purely Satanic than when it rides over the sensibilities of an afflicted conscience, and, selecting the part of greatest tenderness, can feast its eyes over the agonies of the spiritual, even as councils and inquisitors of old did over the agonies of the sentient nature."

In Dr. Chalmers' diary, of this date, the following entry occurs, referring to the arrangement which had been come to:—"Had pretty *tough* work for a time both with M'Leod and with one another, and at length brought him to a declaration by which he compromised no principle whatever, and only acknowledged himself to be wrong in a matter merely legal and *formal*, which he certainly was. This declaration carried him most

triumphantly through the Assembly. The Mode-
rates rejoiced over him as a stray sheep, and we
were all very happy and harmonious on the,
occasion."

The respite in this case afforded much relief to.
the friends of the gospel all over the land ; it.
rejoiced the personal friends of Mr. M'Leod. At
the same time, those who knew him best, and who
could forecast the course likely to be adopted
towards him by his late antagonists, had not much.
hope of a permanent state of peace. No prospect
whatever existed that Mr. M'Leod would change
his principle of action, or his practice in the
matter of the ordinances. In case he did not, it
was anticipated that fresh occasion would be found
against him ; and as the animosity of his colleagues,
though for a time allayed, was not annihilated, a
recurrence of trouble was foreboded.

So accordingly it came to pass. " The clouds
returned after the rain." New complaints were
heard that the ordinances were neglected and dis-'
regarded. The evil was exclaimed against, and
was all traced to the obstinacy or peculiar views
of our friend. No one, at a distance at least,
supposed that any explanation of the anomalous
state of things in *Skye* could be given, or even
existed, save what centred in the person of Mr.

Rory. It was all his doing. The Assembly of 1834, as the practical result of this, had laid on its table a petition from *Skye*, embodying a formal complaint to the above effect, and it then began to be once more a general feeling that interference on the part of the Church was called for. No action, however, was taken on the petition. It was refused, as the petitioners had not submitted it, in the first instance, to the Presbytery. Mr. GRAHAM SPEIRS made the leading speech on the occasion, moving the rejection of the application.

The Assembly of 1835 appointed a Commission to visit the Highlands, to inquire generally into the religious condition of the people, and to report. Though Skye was not *specially* mentioned, it was included in the field to be surveyed ; and there were many of us who believed that the real or chief object in view in the appointment of the Commission was to reach the delinquent of *Bracadale,* and to make an end in some way of this troubler of Israel. This Commission was headed by Sir REGINALD M'DONALD SETON of Staffa, a most honourable man, in whom we had much confidence, and with whom were associated Rev. Dr. Simpson of Kirknewton, Dr. Dewar of Aberdeen, and others.

Their report came up to the Assembly of 1836.

There it ought to have been read and considered in whole. This, for some reason unknown to the general body of the Assembly, was not found to be convenient. In those days reports were not *printed*, as at present, for the use of members in Session, so the contents of the entire Report of the Highland Commission were not known, and we could only guess at the reasons for the course which was actually adopted. No other idea had been previously entertained than that the unfortunate minister of *Bracadale* would be discovered by the Commission to have made his parish the very centre of a widespread departure from even the decencies of Christianity, and that to him would be traced the *whole* defection from *ordinances* (meaning thereby Baptism and the Lord's Supper) which distinguished a large portion of the population of *Skye*. The surmise was, that this expectation had been disappointed, and that the leaders of the day thought it better not to allow the fact to go abroad. The strange procedure accordingly was adopted of deferring the consideration of the Report of the Highland Commission on all the districts which had been visited by them, except one—and that one was not the Isle of Skye itself, but the *parish of Bracadale* only!

Mr. M'Leod and his friends in the Assembly felt

this to be unfair. They felt it to be such a course as would prevent the ends of justice. The case of *Bracadale*, they held, as to the question at issue, could not be impartially judged of save in view of the general condition of almost all the parishes in *Skye*. This they urged as strongly as they could. Very considerable ardour was shown by us. But we were overruled, and it was resolved that the report should be taken up only in the portion of it which referred to *Bracadale*.

Being a member of Assembly, I felt roused by this unfairness, and was moved to attempt some defence in behalf of a brother, although at that time I knew him but slightly. I also sought to defend the interests of evangelical religion in the district with which he was connected, and in which he had been so eminently useful. Ten years dim recollections, and what had occurred through the influence of Dr. Chalmers in 1827 was but partially present to the minds of the members of Assembly of 1836. I went to friends then in Edinburgh, and represented to them that Mr. M'Leod had scarcely ever been dealt with in the way which was most likely to prevail with him, and to serve the cause of truth and righteousness. I urged that he had almost always been treated as a man who was so unmistakably wrong, that he must be hunted down ; that he had always been compelled to stand upon his defence, and to fight for very existence ; but that, if he were dealt with in a friendly spirit, he might yield to friendly communing that which he would never yield to hostile debate and unjustifiable judicia_ decisions.

A large committee of the Assembly was named to prepare, and to lay before the house, that part of the Report on the Highlands which referred to Skye and to Mr. M'Leod. I was put upon this committee, and did my best at our sittings to inoculate with my views all its members. They seemed to concur—especially when I had spoken to them separately—and to be brought the length of being willing to try the experiment of an exclusively friendly Commission, to deal with the whole case of *Bracadale*. I endeavoured to impress them with the view, that if even one member of the Commission to be appointed should be hostile to Mr. M'Leod—known, or by him suspected to be so, or to be under the influence of his pristine pursuers—the object proposed could hardly be expected to be gained. He would still, in that case, preserve the attitude of defence, or even of defiance, and would not permit us to approach him for the purpose of conciliation.

It seemed to me, and to the friends who concurred with me in this view, that we had succeeded in our canvass. The *Moderate* party were not now so omnipotent as they once were. Moreover, a sentiment had begun to establish itself in their minds that it might be well, by some expedient which might be feasible, to put an end to the war which had raged, almost without intermission, in the Presbytery of Skye, and which seemed to justify Mr. Cockburn's assertion, when pleading Mr. M'Leod's cause at the bar of the Assembly, that his Presbytery seemed to keep Mr. Rory as a *bagged fox*, which they let loose when they wished to have a *run*. In view of this, the proposal which had been submitted to the committee did not, upon the whole, seem unreasonable.

It was now considered necessary that Mr. M'Leod should be persuaded to accept the proposed arrangement—the object being conciliation as well as upright action. That he might be prevailed on to accede, and that he might have no suspicion of doubtful or double dealing, I consulted him privately as to the constitution of the intended Commission, who were, in some sense, to judge of his cause, and determine therein for him. The end contemplated was to gain our brother; and, by conciliatory means, to induce him for the future to act in the matter of dispensing sealing ordinances in accordance with the usual practice of the Church. After full conference, he expressed himself satisfied, and accepted the overture thus made to him, so that everything seemed to promise success and ultimate peace. The list of the names for the proposed Commission thus prepared was read in our Assembly's committee, and seemed to be approved of as having been selected in accordance with the plan of procedure, which we had all supposed had been acceded to—no doubt as a matter of much favour to our brother of *Bracadale.*

When the time came, Dr. Simpson read the Report of this Committee in the Assembly. It was all that we had resolved on, until he came to read the *names* of those who were to constitute the Commission. To my dismay, these were wholly changed, so changed, as to entirely subvert the method of action on which we had calculated, and from which we had expected so much, and to destroy the happy prospects I and others had begun to cherish. The change had been made, not in the committee, but out of it. No notice of any change had been given to myself and those acting with me. So far as I could ever learn, no one, but those who were in the secret, had received any intimation of

what had been done, until the report was read to
be approved of by the Assembly ; and then, just
as if, compared with the report itself, the *names*
of the Commission were of no importance, they
were announced with the most perfect *sang froid*,
as if they had been agreed to, and were understood
to be so by all the committee ! It was a dexterous
piece of management ; but I did not think it very
creditable, and certainly it was not in the interests
of peace. I attempted to remonstrate : I told Dr.
Simpson they were not the names agreed to in
committee ; and not the names which had received
the expression of Mr. M'Leod's satisfaction ; not
the names for which we had, virtually, pledged
ourselves to him ; and not the names of persons
in whom either he or his friends could have confidence that they would work *bona fide* in the
direction contemplated—viz. that of conciliatory
dealing with a brother who had been, or conceived
himself to have been, badgered by the Church
Courts for more than twenty years ; but with
whom we had, at last, as I and others understood,
agreed to make the experiment of a new manner
of treatment. In reply, I was coolly told that *no*
names had been *finally* agreed to in committee ;
and, at the same time, I was asked whether I
thought an accused party should be allowed to

K

choose his own judges? My rejoinder was, that the names read in committee, and believed to be agreed to, were *not* names chosen by Mr. M'Leod.

In this transaction I had a specimen of *Moderate* tactics--a transaction in which an understanding which had been clearly come to, for reasons that approved themselves to all before whom they were laid, was set aside, and all remonstrance disregarded.

But who had made the change in the list of names? Of this we never received certain information. But we were told that the original list had been submitted to the Moderator! The Moderator, for the time, was the first Dr. Norman M'Leod, the cousin of our friend. All the world knows that, with some men, attachment to *party* is a stronger principle than love of *kin;* and, aware of the Moderator's proclivities, we never had much difficulty in satisfying ourselves as to who made the change.

Mr. M'Leod at once declared that faith had not been kept with him; and refused to view the Commission but as composed of, at least, as many prejudiced and hostile members, as there were unprejudiced and friendly. He had good reason, as I too well knew, for holding this conviction. It was wonderful, under the circumstances, that my name was retained. Considering the efforts I had been making, perhaps it would have been too much to exclude it. That might have created unpleasant remarks. Whatever the explanation, my name stood among the others as a member of the Commission. Dr. Dewar of Aberdeen was made *Convener*.

Our powers were ample. We were required to meet at *Bracadale* once in the quarter. We were empowered to dispense the ordinances at our discretion. It was part of our duty to give the minister the opportunity of doing so under our direction, and, if he declined, to see that they were dispensed by ourselves, or by others. Our first meeting was to be held at an early day.

When the time approached (just on the eve of the day of meeting) I received a letter, at Glenelg, from Dr. Dewar, our convener, informing me that he could not be present. He at the same time formally nominated me to act as convener for him. There was no public provision in those days for outlay incurred in fulfilling the injunctions of our Superior Courts. It was well, in these circumstances, that there was no penalty exacted for coming short in such fulfilment.

Hitherto my acquaintance with Mr. M'Leod had been limited. I had had but few opportunities of meeting with him ; had never been at *Braca-dale ;* and had never heard him preach. The *out-cry* against him, among one class, in Skye and elsewhere, I had heard, as every one had. Much of that I had ascribed to the hostility among this class against evangelical religion, and to prejudices which had been originated and fostered by that cause. Whilst believing him to be a truly faithful minister, and whilst knowing that he had been made extensively useful in his native island, where he was the centre and soul of all the godly people, I could not divest myself of the feeling that he was to be blamed, perhaps much blamed, for the condition of things prevailing in Skye. The actual state of the case I knew not at this time ; and from all I had heard — all that had been spoken in public and all that had been printed — I expected to meet with the expression of much strong feeling, and with a really public demonstration against him, from the determination to make an end of evils which had elicited so much clamour, and occasioned so much trouble for so long a time within our Church.

The Commission met at Bracadale on 13th July 1836. *Three* members only appeared — a bare *quorum ;* the question of expense having had, naturally enough, its effect. The distances requiring to be travelled were great. I preached to a full congregation, and gave all the intimations required, with a view to our proceeding on our great work in regular order, as became a body representing the august Supreme Court of the Established Church of Scotland. It was intended that we should make the occasion imposing; how far we succeeded it may be difficult to determine.

Presuming on Mr. M'Leod's hospitality, and really having no other resource, I had, on the evening which preceded our meeting, made my way, by my own conveyance, up the steep hill ascending from the public road close to the sea-shore, to the manse of *Bracadale*. I found, much to my comfort, that I had been expected. My reception was polite and kind. The minister himself was reserved. He was evidently on his guard, as a man who expected to be, on the morrow, at the bar, and who was bound, therefore, to be on honour with one who had to act as judge in a cause in which he was a party. So I explained to myself his severe reticence on the whole question that was filling my mind—a matter which, from my heart, I desired to conduct, by God's blessing, to a happy close.

Mrs. M'Leod, appeared to me to present an example of Christian courtesy, propriety, and affection.

Never did I see realised in the manner and conduct of any one the description by the Wise Man, as I did in this lady. "She openeth her mouth with wisdom; and in her tongue is the law of kindness." As to her husband "praising her," anything to which he gave expression, either by utterance or gesture during the evening, was in that direction. But the children of the manse chiefly gained my heart, and made me feel " at home " — as much so as if I had been in the house of a near relative. They were many, and they were all young — stout, handsome creatures, mostly girls, from about eight years and under ; rosy and robust, active, as if they had been the cubs of a lion. Whether it was that kind things had been spoken to them of me or not, I cannot tell, but their " attentions " were most marked. They surrounded me *en masse,* got up on my knees, threw their arms round my neck, kissed me, used every art of prattle, and every art expressive of delight, to impress me favourably, and to gain my admiration. They succeeded. I gave them my heart. How could I do otherwise ? In after days, when they were grown up, I was wont to remind them of the scene, as I had sincere pleasure in recalling it. None of us felt ashamed, or looked back to what I have described with any feeling but that of honest satisfaction. I was pleased to have this outlet for my feelings, amidst the reserve, just and proper in itself, on the part of the head of the house. The evening did *not* seem long. The crowning event came with *worship*.

"It is time to get the books, mamma, before the children get sleepy."

"Yes, love; the servants have finished their work in the byre, and the children are all ready."

There was no more frolic. All the youngsters, to the youngest, were furnished with books. It mattered not that the majority had not yet learned to read. They had their *books;* most demurely did they look into them; and most devoutly, judging by their looks, did they set themselves to use them. As to their knowledge of music I speak not. As to their conscientious conviction that it was their solemn duty to *sing*, I became fully assured. Papa gave out the psalm. They all opened their books—some with the right end uppermost, some with the wrong,—it mattered not. They opened their books. Papa "raised the tune,"—in fair enough style in its way. The choristers seemed to give little heed to his well-meant exercise as *leading* them. Each chose the air which was thought most appropriate, and was most admired by the performer. All sang at the very height of their voices. It was literally a "storm of music" that I was privileged to enjoy. Occasionally I was able, amidst the din, to catch the strains of our astute precentor. He seemed to perceive nothing whatever incongruous in the proceeding. On the contrary, satisfaction beamed in all his features—as it did also in the countenance of his amiable partner. As for the servants, of whom there was a host, to them all was as usual; and I could not help being made to feel that I was the only one present who had had any other impression than that of profound pleasure.

I was on the watch to discover the state of mind at the manse in prospect of the work of the succeeding day—whether there was anxiety, alarm, or any purpose of either standing resolutely against the array of accusers I expected to meet, or any inclination to yield, in any degree whatever, to the dreadful outcry with which I expected our Commission would have to deal. I cannot say that I could discover anything on the one side or the other. I was asked to pray when the *singing* and the reading of Scripture were past. I did so; and I endeavoured to make allusion, as wisely as I could, to the onerous and delicate work in prospect, which lay heavily on my mind, and in which I most earnestly desired guidance. This elicited no remark, and I was by-and-by shown gracefully to my bedroom by my host, who looked kindly after my comforts there, but never opened his mouth on his own matters, more than if there had not been in existence anything so portentous, or at least so momentous, as the " Skye Commission !"

Next morning things were precisely in the same state ; and the Commission met, entering on its business in the old parish church, amidst the solemnities I have already referred to.

I have said that our powers were ample. We were to receive all complaints which might be brought forward as to the conduct of the minister; we were to examine into them, and to judge of their merits ; we were to ask Mr. M'Leod to administer the ordinance of baptism in the case of such persons as, though refused by him, we were satisfied were entitled to receive it for their children (and I had anticipated that we should have very much to do in this direction, such had been the amount of accusation against him) ; in case he refused, we were enjoined to do it ourselves. Further, in concert with the office-bearers, we were instructed to give the necessary intimations ; hold all the customary diets of public worship ; and dispense the sacrament of the Lord's Supper to parishioners offering themselves.

What was my amazement (shall I say my secret satisfaction ?), after all the outcry, and all this parade, to find that there was but *one* to complain ! A retired military officer, who had been believed by some to be much concerned in either raising or fomenting the outcry against Mr. Rory, he only made some show of hostility in the form of complaint. But, whatever effects his word had produced at a distance from *Bracadale*, nothing could be more evident than that it had no effect there. Not a soul appeared to prefer a charge against the minister, or to claim " privileges." Two days were occupied by us in the attempt to fulfil our appointment. We made no progress. To whatever it might be ascribed — whatever might be the explanation—the fact was that no accusers, if they existed, would show face. We demanded that everything should be above board—" with open doors ;" and such was the result. The minister sat in his pew awaiting the progress of the case. He was entitled to do so, for virtually he was at the bar. He did not cpen his lips to utter one word ; and his demeanour on the occasion forcibly reminded me of the word applied to him by Dr. Chalmers when he described him as *dour*, meaning thereby a self-possessed, self-reliant, and self-willed man.

It speedily became, to me at least, very evident that if we proceeded to dispense the communion, it would be dumb show, or a burlesque. I gave no countenance to the suggestion that we should ; for I felt that, though there was no prospect of impropriety in the circumstances, an unkindness and an injustice would be done to Mr. M'Leod, as, in so far as the Commission had discovered, no ground really existed to justify such interference with him in his own parish ;—or with his people, by whom he was manifestly greatly beloved.

The course ultimately adopted by the Commission was, to grant, in the case of any who really desired to share in the privileges of the Church, certificates, expressive of our conviction that they were ecclesiastically entitled thereto, thus authorising any of the neighbouring ministers, to whom they might apply, to admit them, without interference or risk of censure. Not more than two or three of such certificates were solicited from us, and only one baptism was celebrated by the Commission.

Another meeting of the Commission was held, before the meeting of the General Assembly, to mature matters for the Supreme Court, and to resolve on the nature of the report which should be given in. Similar facilities, to those afforded to the parishioners of Bracadale on the first occasion on which we visited them, were again presented, and with the same results. No complaints were tabled against the minister, and no action of a hostile nature to him was demanded from us. Nothing had been done, and the Commission had only to report to the Venerable Assembly that so it was.

When this announcement was made, the disappointment of those who hoped for a confirmation of the charges which, for years, had been brought against the character and conduct of this good man was great ; for not only were these charges not confirmed, but, on the contrary, so far as *Bracadale*, Mr. M'Leod's parish, was concerned, the minister was declared to be free from all such charges.

The Commission was reappointed by the Assembly to which they reported (1837), with the same powers as they previously possessed ; some additional members were named, and I was appointed convener.

V.

Although the ecclesiastical proceedings of the Commission of 1836 were virtually abortive, not providing any materials in the *Bracadale Case* for the Assembly of 1837 to pronounce sentence upon, they were, by no means, without important results. A flood of light was thrown on the state of matters in Skye, to me and to others. Much of this came from the conversations and discussions which, in prosecution of our duty, we had held with the parishioners of *Bracadale*. To me still more came from inquiries which, on my own account, I made among the intelligent friends of truth in the district. Many of these were old men, and distinguished for their position as religions men. With them I made it my business to hold communication, and from them I derived information which I had not previously had, and which I knew the Church at large did not possess. The report presented to the Assembly had been meagre; it could not be anything else. But in course of this season, and previous to the meeting of 1838, I embodied in a tract, which was published in Glasgow, the substance of the information which I had acquired. Copies of this I took care to have put into the hands of our leading men, and among the rest Dr. Candlish. Their eyes were opened, as mine had been; and, whether rightly or not, to this I ascribed, as one chief cause, the general change of sentiment which took place with regard to the long-pursued and much-harassed minister whose story I am narrating.

Another event occurred in course of 1837 which tended in the same direction—the direction of bringing this greatly-protracted trouble to a close. The parish of SNIZORT—the native parish of Mr. Rory, the parish in which his father had for many years been minister—became vacant by the removal of Mr. M'Lauchlan, now of Cawdor, to his present parish. The people of Snizort set their hearts on the son of their old minister. Such efforts as they could make to procure his appointment as successor to Mr. M'Lauchlan they made earnestly. Mr. M'Leod set his heart on becoming their minister. There was a mutual attraction, and in this no doubt God's hand was to be seen. Lord Glenelg (the Right Hon. Charles Grant), my patron, was at this time a member of the Government. Snizort was a Crown presentation. To him I made a representation of the case, touching the interests which would be affected by Mr. M'Leod's being appointed to Snizort. The temporal advantages would be nothing ; but the advantages to the peace and comfort of this estimable man, as well as to his ministerial usefulness, would be unspeakable. Lord Glenelg—wise, prudent, and the ardent friend of evangelical religion in the Highlands—apprehended the merits of the case without difficulty. In due time, as the fruit of this and other interest employed, the presentation of Mr. M'Leod to Snizort was issued. The result was virtually to make an end of the *Bracadale* case, so far as Mr. M'Leod was concerned. Still, while his settlement in Snizort had not taken place, and while our Commission existed, we required to deal with it, and we did so, in terms of the instructions under which we were acting.

"The spirit of slumber which pervaded Scotland in the latter portion of the last century exerted its influence most powerfully over the whole of the North-west Highlands. Indeed, the Reformation in those districts was nothing more than a change from the profession of one creed to that of another, according to the views of the proprietors of the soil. It was purely political, and partook of none of the intelligence and preference of truth to papal ignorance and superstition which distinguished that era in the southern and north-eastern counties. Had a pious clergy succeeded their ghostly predecessors, the knowledge of the 'letter' of the truth would, no doubt, have been imparted to the population of the interesting districts in question ; and although they might, notwithstanding, have been left without any remarkable *revivals* of religion, the 'gross darkness,' which for so long a time prevailed, would, in part at least, have been done away. This, however, was not the case."

Thus I wrote in 1837, as the introduction to the tract which, in that year, was issued by a society in Glasgow as No. X. in a series on *Revivals*, and to which I have referred above.

The first disturbance of the "spirit of slumber" in Skye occurred early in this century. It was part of the fruit of the great movement originated by the HALDANES, and maintained for several years by them, their associates and successors—a movement which may truly be said to have been to our beloved land as "life from the dead," for God was signally with its promoters.

The chief result of the labours of their agent, sent to this island, was the saving conversion of DONALD MUNRO. But how great was the result ultimately accomplished by that conversion, looking to what followed!

Donald, in childhood, had been the victim of smallpox, by which he lost his sight. To gain a livelihood, he had learned to play the violin; and, being naturally of a pleasant disposition, his musical qualifications made him a general favourite. Sympathy for him prevailed among all classes—the clergy as well as others. It came to be thought that the office of *Catechist* in his parish (*Portree*), to which a small salary was attached, might, with advantage to his worldly circumstances, be superadded to his professional avocations. The inconsistency, if observed, was overlooked; and the benevolence implied in making provision for Donald, concealed the incongruity of a blind fiddler filling the spiritual office of parochial catechist. The minister favoured him; the people were pleased with the arrangement; a good memory enabled him to possess himself of all the Shorter Catechism, with several chapters of the New Testament;—so that his qualifications for the discharge of the duties of the office to which he had been promoted were held to be all that were required.

His official character led Donald to hear the itinerant missionary. It was the turning point in his history. "To me that man was a messenger from God," he afterwards declared. "I got new views of Scripture truths, new views of myself, and of the practices of the inhabitants of the island. And the light which I received I dared not put under a bushel."

The catechist of *Portree* was no longer a pluralist. To the work of his *office* he now gave himself exclusively, as one who felt commissioned by an authority higher than that of man, and his ministry was wonderfully blessed of God. He was made the means of the conversion of many. This was the beginning of the revival in *Skye*— a revival genuine, extensive, and followed by abounding fruits of Divine grace ; a revival, moreover, which, though to be traced very much to the agency of those who were not officially in the ministry, embraced, notwithstanding, the effective co-operation of two of the parochial clergy, who were greatly honoured, if not as the originators of the *awakening*, certainly as its friends, —as cherishing, promoting, and advancing it.

For about two years the awakening was general. It began in the parish of *Kilmuir*, extended to *Snizort*, to *Bracadale*, to *Duirnish*—all contiguous parishes. Wherever DONALD MUNRO proceeded, power was made to follow his ministrations. Many who by him came to know the truth returned to their homes in every part of the island, carrying with them the knowledge of the "unsearchable riches of Christ" as great store, and spreading abroad the intelligence of the things which they had seen and heard.

The usual effects in such cases followed : *First*, many were brought to the obedience of the truth as it is in Jesus. *Secondly*, there was an extensive suppression of the openly sinful practices common in the country. *Thirdly*, a large body was formed, whose religion, instead of being a reflection of the image of Christ, was no more than a reflection of that of his people—the work in whom was not of God, but of man; shortcomings in whom gave a handle in a few instances to enemies, who were but too ready, as has always occurred in such cases, to use it to decry the genuine work which had been produced in so many. They were the *tares* which the enemy had sown. *Fourthly*, there followed, from this vital moment, *that* abandonment of ordinances as administered by the parochial clergy, which attracted the attention of the Church, so long disturbed it, and which led to the present Commission. All the professors of religion —real converts, and others—remained devotedly attached to the National Establishment, and resisted efforts made to turn them aside. But the evident divine acknowledgment of DONALD MUNRO's *meetings*, and others of the same character, attracted the people to them, and secured their reverence for the services there conducted. The churches were, in consequence, very much forsaken. The clergy began to refuse sealing ordinances to those who did not attend their ministry —a thing not to be wondered at; and, on the other hand, the " professors " lifted up their protest against the clergy, by *refusing to accept* ordinances as by *them* administered. Hence, in course of time, it ceased to be matter of reproach to live in non-enjoyment of the ordinances. More than this, it came to be counted an evidence of seriousness not to apply to the clergy, and a mark of carelessness or of want of religion on the part of those who made such application, or who received the administration of the ordinances at their hands. So it came to pass that, in the bosom of the Church, we had the anomalous state of things of a large body of professing Christians, distinguished for the fervency of their piety, the purity of their lives, and the warmth of their attachment to her constitution, still maintaining their connection with her, under the deprivation of ordinances for which they earnestly longed; receiving them, when permitted to do so, if administered by those of whom they approved, and with whom, they conceived, they could hold Christian communion; justifying separation, not from the Church, but from her ordinances, on the ground of their *alleged* prostitution by those who ought to have been the guardians of their purity.

The question with which our Commission had to deal, when seen in the light thus presented, was no easy one—a truth which my researches into the history of this case made me to feel most acutely, and, for a time, which almost paralysed my action in the matter.

Mr. Roderick M'Leod's conversion to the Lord was one of the effects of the Skye revival. As the minister of a mission-station, on the Royal Bounty, in the neighbourhood of *Kilmuir*, he had for a few years filled the office, without possessing the spirit, or doing the work, of an evangelist. But, when it pleased God "to call him by his grace, and to reveal his Son in him,"—so preparing and qualifying him for his future course of great usefulness in the Church—it was no longer so with him. Then to the service of the Gospel he gave himself, "soul, body, and spirit." With his change of views and practice as a minister of the New Testament, he adopted the sentiments prevalent among the religious people of the country on the question regarding the ordinances, those who were entitled to administer them, and those who ought to be admitted to share in them. His unflinching (I do not say intelligent) adherence to those views, and, consequently, his unusual strictness in the rule of admission, soon involved him in the trouble which, in church courts and otherwise, he for so long a time suffered—trouble, the enduring of which greatly endeared him to all those in the country who had turned from their idols to serve the living

God. If anything could have succeeded in separating for ever from our Church this valuable body of devoted adherents, it would have been the deposition of this estimable man. In the good providence of God this was averted—a result, under Him, to be ascribed to the work of the *Skye* Commission, for the part I was enabled to take in which I praise and thank His name.

Mr. M'Leod was not the cause of the disorders which prevailed in *Skye*. Cruelly was he charged with being so, and long was he the object of persecution on that account by enemies, as well as the object of suspicion by those who were *his* friends, and the friends of truth. These, so far as I know, never justified him in adopting the views which he did, and in acting so determinedly on them. But when they came to understand his position, they extended to him their sympathy, their forbearance, and friendliness, in every competent form. He was the *victim* of the erroneous views which had found so strong a place in his country, and not the *cause ;* and practically he really was less guilty than many ministers in his neighbourhood (if I may speak of guilt in such a connection), as to the administration of ordinances in his parish. The Commission found that not in his, but in the parishes of others, the greatest amount of the unbaptized were to be found, as well as of those who were not fully in membership with the Church.

How much it had become a general opinion that Mr. M'Leod was to blame for the evils existing in *Skye*, appears, among other things, by the fact that the Committee of the House of Commons on Sites, in 1847, had been instructed to make this question a subject of examination, as part of their labours ; by whom so instructed, however, I know not. My examination before that Committee was in part directed to it. I was examined thereon, my connection with the Commission being no doubt the cause. Other witnesses were so examined also. The member for the county of Inverness at the time, Mr. Baillie, one of the Committee—a man of different sentiments from the members for the county in my time—took me to task :—

" *Mr. Baillie.*—You state that the people in Skye refused the ordinances in consequence of a revival of religion, in 1812 ?—It began at that time.

" Is the committee to understand that, in your opinion, the refusal to receive the sacrament is a proof of a revival of religion ?—Certainly not ; I do not mean to say that.

" Would you not suppose that, if a man was anxious to receive the sacrament, he was a religious man?—I believe that many men who are not religious are anxious to receive the sacrament.

"You would not consider a man a religious man, if he was anxious to receive the sacrament?—I would not consider his anxiety to receive the sacrament a proof of his being a religious man.

"You stated that when you went to examine the parish of Bracadale you did not find that the refusal of the ordinances was so great in Bracadale parish as in several others?—We found that the number of children regularly baptized in the parish of Bracadale was greater than in some of the neighbouring parishes.

"Are you aware that there were no more than five or ten in the parish of Bracadale, out of a population of 2000, admitted to the ordinances?—I am not aware of that.

"Are you aware that the gentry in the parish, and all their families, were refused the ordinances?—I am not aware of that; it may be true, but I did not know it; I knew that such allegations were made.

"Were these allegations investigated by the deputation of which you formed a part?—I do not think that we made any distinction between the gentry and others.

"But did you investigate the accusations generally?—The accusations generally were as to refusal of ordinances; and we inquired into the extent to which it went, and the reason for which the ordinances were refused.

"And you do not remember whether there were only five or ten communicants in the parish of Bracadale?—No, I do not.

"Are you aware that Mr. M'Leod did not administer baptism to the children of any to whom he refused the ordinances?—I know that. Perhaps it may be proper to observe that there are two views held in the Church of Scotland with regard to that matter. Some ministers hold distinctly that the children of no person should be admitted to receive baptism from the ministers of the Church unless he be a communicant or partaker of the Lord's Supper; others are of opinion that baptism may be administered to children of parents who are not communicants. Mr. Roderick M'Leod holds decidedly the view that parents being communicants alone ought to have their children baptized, and he is strict in admitting to the Lord's table; consequently, as he baptizes only the children of those who are partakers at the Lord's table, the number of children baptized by him is small.

" If there were only five or ten communicants in the parish of Bracadale, would you say that any other parish in Skye could be in a worse state than that ?—I cannot speak as to that ; I do not know whether ten or five was the number of communicants there. Perhaps I might be allowed to say that if all indiscriminately were admitted to the Lord's Supper, that would be a much worse state of things than the other, though both may be bad."

VI.

When our report of the second year's proceedings was presented to the Assembly of 1838, I was not there. The heavy affliction which, in the spring and early summer of that year, fell on my family, which I have recorded elsewhere, prevented my attending. What I could do I did— instructing our presbytery elder, Mr. Murray Dunlop, and others, to put the Assembly in possession of the whole case, that they might judge of it. Some discussion ensued, ending in the reappointment of the Commission, with Dr. Grant of Saint Mary's as convener.

Dr. Grant called a meeting somewhat late in the season, but he did not himself attend. When the Commission met I was chosen clerk, and all the papers in the case remained in my charge. It was, however, no longer a Commission to deal with the case of *Bracadale*. We had by this time got into a wider field. Our convener, in a letter somewhat pretentious, instructed us that our duty, under the remit of the General Assembly—a remit which he did not think embraced all that it ought to have done—was to consider the state of matters in the country generally, and, if possible, to devise and suggest the remedy which should be adopted. I kept him regularly informed of all our proceedings. He had extracts from the minutes of our meetings sufficient for fully informing him of all the Commission did, as well as of the order of our proceedings. His report to the Assembly of 1839 showed that he had received, and had, adopted, information resting on other authority, and on evidence other than that of the Commission of Assembly, and that he had given effect to it in a form by which I felt aggrieved. I was not present, however, and the matter was allowed to pass. Dr. Grant received the thanks of the Assembly. One man labours, and another enters into his labours !

Dr. Grant's convenership lasted for one year only. Dr. Gordon was named his successor. But he never called the Commission together. To the

Assembly of 1840 he, however, read a report which contained some able discussion, bearing, of course, on Mr. M'Leod's views indirectly, but ending in no conclusions requiring further action on the part of the Church.

So terminated this long-continued controversy. No more was heard of the dreadful condition of things in *Skye*. Mr. Rory was at peace "among his own people" in Snizort, prosecuting an active and a successful ministry. In a very few short years our great Disruption came. No man of us met it with so light a heart as our long-tried friend. "This," he said to me on the occasion, "is what my mind was made familiar with for many a year. My chief terror then was that I should be alone in the separation; but now I am where I then looked to be, and with nearly 500 of my brethren by my side!" The gigantic efforts which at the Disruption he was called to make in his native island all the Church at the time knew, as they admired them. Alone in *Skye* for a time, for he was the only one of his presbytery who "came out," his services of ministry were bestowed everywhere. Mordecai was exalted. In all the years from that period, till his death, he lived honoured, beloved, almost revered. It was a thing beseeming his position in the Church, his

apostolic character, his eminent gifts as a herald of
the everlasting Gospel, and the divine favour which
he had for a long life enjoyed, that he should be
raised to the Moderator's chair of the Free Church.
This was done, to the delight of thousands, in
1863; and the talent which his appearances in
that capacity showed surprised not a few, although
none certainly of those who were his intimates.
When he died in 1867 there was a great mourning,
such as *Skye*, perhaps, never witnessed before.
An affecting circumstance it was, that his loving
parishioners would permit the use of no hearse,
nor other conveyance, in bearing his mortal
remains to their long home. On their own
shoulders, one relay after another, they carried
him, as if in charge of a precious treasure, and
laid him in the " narrow house" amidst a grief
most affecting because it was real—every one as if
under the power of the spirit of the prophet when
he exclaimed, " My Father! my Father! the
chariot of Israel and the horsemen thereof." I
loved him for his genuine worth. He was a real
man—*justum et tenacem propositi virum*—" Stead-
fast, unmovable, ever abounding in the work of
the Lord."

Of his large family four only remain—two sons,
in India; two daughters, not in robust health,

sojourning on the Continent. Two of his daughters —attractive creatures they were—who died at *Bridge of Allan,* sleep in my family burying-ground at Stirling. A son, a youth of uncommon promise, died at *Pau,* in the south of France. From his grave, in the cemetery there, I plucked a beautiful little rosebud in the early summer of 1863, and sent it by post to his father. He received the letter in which it was enclosed, in the Moderator's chair, when presiding over the deliberations of the Assembly ; and more beautiful, he told me, it was in his eyes than all the gorgeous bouquets which, day by day, through the kindness of admirers, graced his table.

Mr. M'Leod in stature was not above the ordinary height. His habit of body tended to corpulency. He was singularly abstinent and temperate. In speech he was slow and deliberate, never almost being known to utter a rash or un-advised word. His voice was sweet and mellow. In the pulpit he was calm in a degree that seemed to forbid effect. Yet, such was the elegance of his diction, especially in the use of the Gaelic language ; such the graceful selection and original application of Scriptural quotations, and the un-affected and quiet pathos which breathed in all he said; such the love for souls and desire for the glory of his Master that beamed in his eyes and in all his features, that seldom has there been a preacher who so entirely took possession of his hearers, carrying mind, and heart, and all, with him. His name must ever be mentioned among the first of the worthies of the Highlands in recent times.

I cannot omit to say that of those who sympathised with me, stood by me, and aided me by their countenance and support, one esteemed friend remains till this day. I refer to Mr. Colin M'Kenzie, then minister at *Shieldag*, presbytery of Lochcarron; lately Free Church minister at *Arrochar*, Dumbartonshire; and now a respected and venerable member of my congregation at Stirling. His consistency and upright course through a long life devoted to the service of the Master in heaven is now his " good report."

Here ends the story of Mr. Rory and the BRACADALE CASE.

VII.

It is time that I should return to the narrative of our *Highland Tour*. We are still at SLIGEACHAN HOTEL. The wanderers on the moor have enjoyed a satisfactory night's rest. Early morning of the 14th August has come. The fishermen have had a successful night's work; and when our party assemble at the breakfast table they are regaled with herrings, both boiled herrings and fried, of the first quality—not of the draught, selections from which, the evening preceding, had been so acceptable, but herrings which, a few hours back, had been disporting themselves "all alive" in the wide sea. The accompaniments on the occasion are worthy of the principal dish. We have a journey and work in prospect for the day, a fact, the anticipation of which leads to a generous, if not too generous, use of the Highland luxuries provided for us.

We were soon on the road. Our first halt was to be made at *Bracadale,* where we were expected, as we had weeks before been announced. Two conveyances were provided. It was arranged that one should be occupied by the ministers of St. George's, Edinburgh, and of Snizort. The other was assigned to me and a travelling companion, who was to accompany us for the day. Mr. Rory was celebrated for his knowledge of horses, and for his taste in all sorts of vehicles. He drove the best ponies, finely harnessed to the most tasteful carriages, in Skye. Thus, as to the means of transit, we were all most comfortably accommodated. The sun shone brilliantly. All the dark shadow of clouds. which had made our journey from *Strathaird* to *Sligeachan* so dismal, had disappeared; the road was smooth as a garden walk; in short, we were buoyant and pleased with everything for the time.

At *Bracadale* we had our usual services. Dr. Candlish and I both preached—he, of course, in English, and I "in the other language." Mr. M'Leod would not take any part of the work. There were several things to arrange here, as in every place we visited. In this department of of our duty Mr. M'Leod was of much service. His approval of our appointments seemed to satisfy all concerned.

I had not been at *Bracadale* since the famous days of the Skye Commission. The present visit brought back to my mind the painful conflict of ten years before—a conflict for the right; but a conflict which entailed on me, for the time, much unpopularity. Its happy result was my reward. This day, as I witnessed the new order of things in full operation—though we no more ascended the hill to the old hospitable manse—filled my heart with joy. We must wait *for* God, as well as wait *on* Him, if we are to see his faithfulness to his word. "Said I not unto thee, that if thou wouldest believe, thou shouldest see the glory of God?"

From *Bracadale* we proceeded to *Dunvegan*. Our road lay along the sea-coast—an enchanting drive

M

—affording glimpses, in the clear sunshine, of the far distant islands and the nearer islets of this margin of the great Atlantic. We had on the preceding evening seen them under one aspect, from the heights to the west above *Strathaird;* we saw them now under another aspect. On both occasions we were enraptured with the scenery of sea and land alike.

Our services at *Dunvegan* were the same as they had been at *Bracadale* and the other places we had visited. We preached, and made such arrangements as were required, and as we were expected to make during this tour, for the comfortable ordering of matters in the prosecution of local ministerial and evangelistic work.

The journey which we had accomplished since morning (of about twenty-four miles), besides our labour of speech, with the fatigue of our previous night's adventure not yet entirely subsided, made us very ready for our night's repose.

Our arrival and work at *Dunvegan* were made very enjoyable, as Dr. M'Kellar rejoined our party at this place. He had come to *Skye* by a different route from ours, and had taken his share of deputation labours in localities which we had not been able to visit.

The romantic castle of *Dunvegan,* with its environs, marked with the traces of àntiquity, arrests every traveller's eye. Could Scott have had it before him when he described the ruin of Ellangowan? "Situated upon a promontory or projection of rock which formed one side of a small and placid bay on the sea-shore, the ground behind descending to the sea by a small swelling green bank, divided into levels by natural terraces, on which grew some old trees, and terminating upon the white sand. The other side of the bay, opposite to the old castle, was a sloping and varied promontory, covered chiefly with copsewood, which on that favoured coast grows almost within watermark. The grey old towers of the castle, partly entire, partly broken, here bearing the rusty weather-stains of ages, and there partially mantled with ivy, stretched along the verge of the dark rock which rose on the right hand. In front was the quiet bay, whose little waves, crisping and sparkling to the moonbeams, rolled successively along its surface, and dashed with a soft and murmuring ripple against the silvery beach."

Dr. Samuel Johnson's description, written in 1773, occurring in the account of his Journey to the Western Highlands, may be placed side by side with this. He says —

" *Dunvegan* is a rocky prominence, that juts out

into a bay on the west side of *Skye*. The house, which is the principal seat of the Macleods, is partly old and partly modern ; it is built upon the rock, and looks upon the water. It forms two sides of a small square ; on the third side is a skeleton of a castle of unknown antiquity, supposed to have been a Norwegian fabric, when the Danes were masters of the islands. It is so nearly entire, that it might have easily been made habitable, were there not an ominous tradition in the family that the owner should not long outlive the reparation. The grandfather of the present laird, in defiance of the prediction, began the work, but desisted in a little time, and applied his money to worse uses."

At *Dunvegan* we rested for the night. Next morning, early, saw us on our way to *Snizort*, travelling much in the order of the previous day, —only that I had now as my travelling companion my esteemed friend who had joined us at our last halting-place. The journey to the residence of Mr. M'Leod was one of about eighteen miles ; and our object, this morning, was to arrive there for breakfast, intending thereafter to occupy all our time till evening in the business of his parish and congregation. The Free Church Manse of *Snizort* was not yet built. Our friend lived (having of course quitted the manse, the house in which he had been born, at the Disruption) in a dwelling of small dimensions, on the hillside stretching up from *Loch Snizort,* and in full view of that beautiful sheet of sea. It was a thoroughly occupied house—densely peopled. Our friend's family had then known no break — a family numerous, healthy, contented, and rejoicing.

I had described to Dr. Candlish, in some of our conversations by the way, the *singing* which I anticipated at worship, when we came to *Snizort.* I had narrated my experience in that point at *Bracadale.* He was amused, but accused me of exaggeration. After the arrival of our party, and after a comfortable breakfast was partaken of, furnished by true Highland hospitality, the BOOKS made their appearance. The children and the servants came streaming in — until the apartment was more than filled. The psalm was given out. The head of the family "raised the tune," as I had heard him do before. There was little heed given, as I had formerly witnessed, to his selection, or to his *leading.* The burst of accompaniment, with every variety of selection and intonation, was perfect. I looked towards Dr. M'Kellar : most grave, with downcast eyes—but a shade of humour playing on his features—was his countenance. A hurried glance which Dr. Candlish cast satisfied me that he would not again accuse me of exaggeration. No one but ourselves seemed in the least to notice what affected us. Dr. M'Kellar led, with great feeling, in prayer.

Before entering on our work for the day, the visitors strolled along the slopes of the hill on which the house stood. The *singing*, for a moment, became the subject of conversation.

"You did right to forewarn me," said Dr. Candlish; "but was it not *fine?*"

"Well, well; *Non clamans sed amans*," remarked Dr. M'Kellar.

"*Et amans et clamans*," was the reply; and then, after a short pause, the supplement—

"*Sonat in aure Dei.*"

Often in subsequent years would Dr. Candlish refer to the scene, with the remark, "Oh, do you remember the singing at Mr. Rory's?"

Our excursion on the hill-side over, we repaired to the huge fabric of a church which had been built for the accommodation of our friend's congregation. The multitude assembled was very great. Mr. M'Leod was not now merely the minister of Snizort. Past boundaries were thrown down; former restrictions no longer had force. He was, at this date, virtually the *Bishop of Skye.*

Snizort was a grand centre. Hither the friends of the good cause gathered themselves—on Sabbath days for worship, at other times for counsel and direction. Thus the end of all the conflicts our friend had endured, was his exaltation to a position of eminence and unchallenged influence in the ecclesiastical world of this whole region. Who could deny that he was worthy of it? His genuine piety, his zeal, his uprightness, his earnest devotedness of heart and life, his great natural talent and sagacity, coupled with singular prudence, made him so. Not that those who loved him for his virtues were blind to his faults; not that they justified him, or felt they could defend him, as to his views concerning the sealing ordinances of the Church—views on which he doggedly persisted to act, though, we had reason to believe, in a modified degree, in his later years; but, taking him all in all, making due allowances for his infirmities and idiosyncrasies, he must be held to have been worthy of the place which, by almost universal consent, was awarded him throughout *Skye*, and in the Highlands generally.

The public services in the church, on this day, were conducted in the same order we had followed in other places. We had preaching in Gaelic and in English, as in other cases—the former falling to me, the latter to Dr. Candlish, for Dr. M'Kellar thought it advisable not to supersede Dr. Candlish ; and his Gaelic had departed from him, so that he could not take my place.

The services past, there were many references, touching matters affecting various congregations, either settled or that looked for speedy settlement, with which we had to deal. Every one of them received due consideration, as all similar references, at the various stations we had visited on our way, had done. Much good was, in this way, accomplished by our visits, and much satisfaction and contentment were made to prevail; whilst our minds were stored with information of great importance, in view of future legislation and action as to this section of the Highlands.

At the close of a laborious but happy day, Dr. M'Kellar, Dr. Candlish, and I, proceeded, by Mr. Rory's conveyance, to *Portree*. Late in the evening we embarked on board the *Breadalbane* Free Church yacht, which had been ordered to meet us there—part of the long past pre-arrangements— and which awaited our arrival. In her we slept, and slept comfortably, for the night.

I may be permitted a sentence or two about the YACHT. The idea of having such an appendage to' our Free Church accommodation received much favour from Dr. M'Kellar, if it did not originate with him. He and other friends were of the opinion that, besides affording facilities for visiting the Highlands in all directions, the *prestige* of such an institution would tell greatly in our favour in the Highland mind generally. Others were not of the same opinion ; but believed that, being a *sailing* vessel, not a *steam* ship, depending on winds and weather, whilst time required to be kept with assembled expectant congregations, the *Yacht* would often create disappointments, and might seriously interfere with successful action in our work. Moreover, though the original cost had been defrayed by private subscription, the expense of maintaining her in commission all the year round was very considerable. After a time, accordingly, the *Breadalbane* was disposed of, though to the regret of many.

She was a small vessel—of about thirty tons register—schooner rigged, of great sailing virtue, and safe as any sailing vessel could be. Employed, on one occasion, to convey some one of our deputations up the Mediterranean, she crossed the Bay of Biscay in a gale, and with a sea running in which large war-ships were rolling to and fro, dipping their yards in the huge waves as every sea came on them, each making a clean breach over their hulls, whilst the BREADALBANE floated like a duck on the top of the waves, and sped on her way, not shipping a drop of water! Such was the report which those who sailed in her gave of her merits as a *sea-boat*, on their return.

Her *name* was given to her in honour of the noble friend of our Church, the late Marquess of Breadalbane. How much this nobleman lived in the hearts of all true Free Churchmen, his contemporaries know; and how worthy he was that it should do so—not for his rank only, but for the intelligent apprehension of the great questions which had agitated our Church, the principles for the integrity of which we had contended, and for the conservation of which we had, for the time, suffered—his intelligent apprehension, and his bold and manly advocacy of these, in face of the great opposition offered to them by his peers in the House of Lords; ultimately his *coming out*, as the ministers and as other elders did; and then bestowing his bounteous gifts, affording facilities for rendering our Free Church, over his wide and extensive property, a permanent institution. His distinguished coadjutor in all such testimony and effort, the Hon. Fox Maule, now the Earl of Dalhousie, was to the Free Church, in the Lower House, what the Marquess was in the Upper House of Parliament.   Mr. Fox Maule was even more to us than what the Marquess was, because of the *arena* in which he then had his place, and also because of his high-styled eloquence. DALHOUSIE still remains with us (may God long spare him!), and shares in our debates in the General Assembly, affording a very gratifying illustration —in which he seems to delight—of Presbyterian parity ; assuming no influence among us but what his skill and talent in apprehending the questions which come before us, his clearness of statement when he speaks, and his masterly power of debate, entitle him to.

With the Marquess of Breadalbane, I had the honour of being acquainted from his college days at the Glasgow University, where, as students, we were contemporaries.   In 1826, when I was minister of Hope Street Chapel, Glasgow, he presented me to the parish of Kilbrandon, Argyleshire (he did so, virtually, though his father was then alive) ; and, during life, he was my friend, showing me much kindness.   I last met him at Oban in 1862, shortly before his untimely death.   One little incident I record to show the kindliness of his disposition.   On the day after my arrival, I chanced to see him on the street, surrounded by a group of county gentlemen. I went up and spoke to him. He received me kindly. After a little he separated from the gentlemen with whom he had been engaged, took my arm, and led me along the street.

"Do you know *our* minister here?" He meant the Free Church minister.

"I know him very well. You mean Mr. Cameron, my lord?"

"Yes. I wish to call for him at his manse, if you would kindly accompany me."

Of course I did. The visit was a great occasion there. Everything was nice and tidy. The children greatly attracted the distinguished visitor: he fondled them, and they, not knowing the distinction between the great man and the others present, were frank with him, receiving his attentions with evident satisfaction, and warmly returning them in their own way. After inquiries as to the manse and church accommodation (both being on his lordship's property), and inviting the minister, if he wished for anything additional, to let him know, we took our leave.

On the Sabbath he asked my wife and myself to accompany him to his pew in the Free Church, which we did. He placed her at the upper part of the seat, where he sat beside her, giving me my place on his other hand. It was intended as a

mark of attention to us—putting honour on us
before the people—in the place of my wife's birth
and upbringing, and where I had laboured, as he
knew, for the first four years of my ministry. By
such acts of condescending kindness, how much
do persons of rank, holding eminent positions in
society, procure respect for themselves and good
will for their social distinctions!

The night's repose on board the *Breadalbane*
greatly refreshed us ; and so, especially, did our
sail thereafter. The anchor was early up, and we
were under weigh with the dawn of morning. Our
destination, in the first instance, was *Broadford*.
There, at *one* o'clock, we were expected to conduct such services as had been conducted at the
various places of halt, during our entire progress.
For such services we had been announced at
Broadford, as pre-arranged. The weather was
fine, bright and bracing as an autumn day ; the
tide was favourable ; the scenery delightsome ;
and, though we felt the disadvantages of a *sailing*
as compared with a *steam* propelled vessel, in
respect of rapidity of motion and prospective pre-
cision in time-keeping, we nevertheless, under
present circumstances, cherished every hope that
we should make good our object.

Part of our voyage lay through the sound of *Raasay*—the island of *Raasay* being on our left, and the coast of *Skye* on the right. The herring-fishing was at its best, and the liveliness which boats, nets, men, women, and children, along both shores, gave to the scene, as the proceeds of the night's toil were landed and rejoiced over by the expectant throng, was very cheering. It was impossible to skirt along the coast of this island, and not have the great moralist and his "Journey" of nearly sixty years before, brought to mind, especially his visit to *Raasay*. We talked of the record of it which he has left to the world. We could remember some portions, though not all, of what he had written. Often as the celebrated passage about *Iona* has been quoted, I know not that its beauty exceeds that of the sentences which he penned about *Raasay* :—

"Our reception exceeded our expectations. We found nothing but civility, elegance, and plenty. After the usual refreshments, and the usual conversation, the evening came upon us. The carpet was then rolled off the floor, the musician was called, and the whole company was invited to dance, nor did ever fairies trip with greater alacrity. The general air of festivity which predominated in this place, so far remote from all those regions which the mind has been used to contemplate as the mansions of pleasure, struck the imagination with a delightful surprise, analogous to that which is felt at an unexpected emersion from darkness to light. *Raasay* has little that can detain a traveller, except the laird and his family; but their power wants no auxiliaries. Such a seat of hospitality, amidst the winds and waters, fills the imagination with a delightful contrariety of images. Without is the rough ocean and the rocky land, the beating billows and the howling storm; within is plenty and elegance, beauty and gaiety, the song and the dance. In *Raasay*, if I could have found an *Ulysses*, I had fancied a *Phœocia*."

In my Glenelg days—I was able to tell my friends—I occasionally called at the house of *Ardintoul*, on the coast immediately opposite to *Lochalsh*. Bad weather often forced me to take the circuitous route by the ferry of *Totaig*, that I might land on the *Glenelg* side. *Ardintoul* was the residence of Mrs. M'Rae, mother of one of Wellington's celebrated officers, knighted for his gallantry, and in my time known as Sir John M'Rae. Mrs. M'Rae was a daughter of M'Leod of *Raasay*—*the* M'Leod whose hospitality Dr. Johnson celebrates. The old lady was, at the time of the great man's visit, a young maiden, one of those whom he saw dance, and whom he admired. She delighted to speak of him, and was always anxious to dispel the prejudices which so many Highlanders have entertained towards Johnson for his work on the Highlands. Even in old age she appeared beautiful—tall, and elegant in her manners.

We were landed comfortably on the shore at *Broadford* in due time. The multitude was assembled to meet and to welcome us. No delay required to be made. I preached first in the mountain tongue, and whilst so engaged my companions strolled along the sea rocks, which in this locality are of much interest to those who know anything of geology and its discoveries, so occupying the leisure hour which my engagement afforded them. The other part of our prescribed duty, in English, was conducted, as usual, by Dr. Candlish. Business matters connected with the affairs of our Church in this district followed, and we were soon ready to pursue our voyage, our destination for the night being *Balmacara*, and the hospitable mansion of our good friend, Mr. Lillingston.

At *Broadford* we were on the property of a site-refusing landlord, Lord M'Donald. Mr. M'Kinnon, *Corry*, was his factor. He had been an acquaintance of mine in my Glenelg days, and my impression of his character was that he knew better than to pursue *ex animo* the course which he now did. Accompanied by Dr. Candlish, I called on him. He was pleased, and seemed flattered even, with our visit. Had he been free from the prejudices which his position and office, I may say, compelled him to cherish and obey, he might have been turned to some measure of friendliness. I never learned, however, that our visit, though intended for good, produced any marked effect.

He was one of the witnesses who, in 1847, were examined by the Committee of the House of Commons on Sites. His evidence furnishes for contemplation a melancholy example of the conduct of too many of the Scottish landed proprietors at the period of the Disruption. One or two extracts will show this :—

" *Mr. F. Maule.*—Do the adherents of the Free Church, who are tenants of Lord M'Donald, pay their rents as regularly and as punctually as other parties who are not members of the Free Church ?— They do.

"There are not more arrears on the part of those who belong to the Free Church than there are on the part of others ?—No.

"Have you found that since the Disruption of the

N

Church in Skye you have had greater facility or more difficulty in collecting the arrears due upon the estate ?—I have found no difference ; the people all hold from year to year, and of course they make a point of paying their rents, because their continuance in possession very much depends on their doing so.

"Has it been usual on Lord M'Donald's estate to dispossess tenants for other reasons than non-payment of rents ?—Not without some particular bad conduct or fault.

"Suppose it were necessary to dispossess tenants in order to make improved arrangements with reference to farms, is it usual in Skye to provide for the families who are removed for those purposes, in any way ?—Sometimes it is impracticable ; but, generally speaking, they are provided for, and very often they emigrate.

"When unprovided for, and unable to provide for themselves, what becomes of those people ?—A good many of them emigrate ; but there is not much of the system of dispossessing tenants followed in Skye.

"Since the Disruption in the Church have any ejectments of tenants been made, or have any notices of ejectment been served, for other reasons than non-payment of rents, or non-improvement in the condition of the farms ?—Yes.

" I will read you a list of individuals. In the parish of Kilmuir do you know the following persons :—[Here follows a list of sixteen names, one of the number being a catechist, another a Gaelic school-teacher]. In the parish of Snizort [eight names]. In the parish of Portree [four names]. In the parish of Sleat [five names]. Do you know these individuals?—Of course I know them all when I see them ; but I do not know them by hearing their names read in that way ; at least not the whole of them.

" Have individuals of the names which I have read to you received notices to quit ?—They have, I believe.

" Are you aware whether all those are or are not members of the Free Church ?—I am not aware whether all are ; some of them are not, I should think.

" Will you look at the list, and mention any who are not members of the Free Church ?—I cannot tell you who is not a member. Here is a man, Donald M'Donald, the catechist, he must be a member of the Free Church, because he is not a catechist in the Establishment ; but I cannot tell, with respect to many of the others, which are and which are not members of the Free Church.

" Is Lord M'Donald cognisant of these notices of ejectment upon his property ?—It was he himself gave me the list of such as he wished to be served with notices on account of their being collectors [for the Sustentation Fund].

"Whose advice did he act upon in that matter? —I cannot say.

"He did not act upon your advice?—No; and I do not say that he has made up his mind about removing them, for I have not spoken to him on the subject since I have been here; but the day he was leaving the country he gave me a list, and said—'Here is a list of fellows that must have notice to quit.'

"Do you know Ewen Cameron, an innkeeper in *Uig?*—Yes.

"Was it for arrears or any misconduct that he was ejected at Whitsunday 1846?—No; there were complaints made to Lord M'Donald that he was a strong partisan for the Free Church, and being, as we considered, a public servant, we thought it better to remove him.

"Who are 'We?'—Lord M'Donald and myself.

"Did you suppose that, as an innkeeper, he was likely to refuse accommodation to those who were not of the same Church views as himself?—I do not know that he would refuse accommodation to them, but he would give the preference to his own side," etc. etc. etc.

I met Mr. M'Kinnon in the corridor as he came out from the committee-room. He looked flushed and agitated. "Ah," he said to me, "you have it all your own way here; but wait till we get a hold of you in the country." "Here," I answered, "we get justice, no favour, and we ask no more." The examinations by the site-committee, when they came to be known in the Highlands, did much to encourage and strengthen both ministers and people of the Free Church.

Our sail from *Broadford* to *Lochalsh* and *Balmacara* was pleasant, but without adventure or incident of special interest. Our reception was cordial and sincere. Since we parted with our friends, though the time was not long, we had seen much, and had, as I have already noted, laid up stores of valuable information, whilst we had received impressions of men and of things which we could not have had without personal observation and personal intercourse.

It was now Saturday. The next day was Sabbath, 17th August, when we had onerous duty in prospect; rest and refreshment were needed. Our considerate friends saw this. We were left, accordingly, much to ourselves for the evening. I had feared that ministerial work might have been required, but this was not the case. The repose was really due to us, and due to the work to which we looked forward.

On the morrow, when it came, we had double service—service at two different places, at a considerable distance from each other—at least ten miles. *First* we drove to *Plockton*, accompanied by our friends of *Balmacara* House. Next, coming back, and passing *Balmacara*, we proceeded to *Ardelve*, a station on a branch of *Loch Duich*, called *Lochlong*, on the banks of which stands the village of *Dornie*. The public road passes near to *Ardelve*, where there is a ferry station, the arm of sea stretching between the *Lochalsh* and *Kintail* coasts —*Dornie* being in the district of *Kintail*.

Both at *Plockton* and at *Ardelve* we had very large audiences; especially at the latter place. Here, at the era of the Disruption, Mr. Lillingston had reared an immense fabric, in its construction suited to what, he believed, the exigencies and circumstances of the times required. He intended that the building should be at the service of the *gospel*, not of any special Church, not of the Free Church exclusively, but of any who really declared the truth for the salvation of men. The question of how the character of those professing to proclaim the truth on this principle was to be ascertained he left undecided. The structure was a very un-

gainly one.. Built at a spot where violent torna-
does occasionally came sweeping down from the
neighbouring mountains, he conceived that to give
it a roof elevated in the least would be to expose
it to risk. So the roof was made entirely flat,
except that the smallest possible incline to one
side was provided for, that the rain should run off,
and not lodge anywhere on the vast flat. It was
covered with FELT, which was periodically pitched
with boiled tar. In summer the rays of the sun
produced their proper effect, which was by no
means pleasant to many of the worshippers. The
great bulk being fishermen, and accustomed to
such flavour as abounded there, were not disturbed by it. Dr. Chalmers said of the first Free
Church erected—that which Dr. Candlish's congregation occupied when the Disruption occurred,
and which had been erected in prospect of that
event as temporary accommodation—that it reminded him (the roof being covered with felt) of a
boy *with a scabbed head.* Had he seen the *Ardelve*
church, he probably would have said that it resembled a decapitated giant, of course with no
head at all. All that could be said for it was, that
it afforded an illustration of Mr. Lillingston's notions
of the cheapness, the architectural elegance and
comfort, which it behoved the Free Church to study.

I never on any occasion heard Dr. Candlish preach so admirably, or with such effect. His subject, as I knew, was a favourite one with him : John xxi. 15-17—"So when they had dined, Jesus saith to Simon Peter, Simon, son of Jonas, lovest thou me more than these?" etc. etc. etc. He used no MS.; spoke without a single note of any kind to aid his memory; threw himself freely into his statement of truth; evidently aimed to use language the simplest, clearest, most direct, for making his meaning, in every particular, palpable and unquestionable. Never was he, on any occasion in all his ministry, more successful in arresting and retaining the attention, or in delighting and edifying an audience. The poor people, though their knowledge of English was scanty, nevertheless, to my apprehension, comprehended it all. Having begun the services of the day by preaching in the vernacular, it was my part, in concluding the services, to give, in the said vernacular, a *resumé* of the English discourse. This I found a very easy task, as well as a very delightful one, under the circumstances.

> "Hark, my soul ! it is the Lord,
> 'Tis thy Saviour, hear his word ;
> Jesus speaks, and speaks to thee ;
> Say, poor sinner, lov'st thou Me ?

" Lord ! it is my chief complaint,
    That my love is weak and faint ;
    Yet I love Thee and adore !
    O for grace to love Thee more !"—*Cowper.*

All were charmed. This may have arisen in part, as often happens, from the audience having been prepared—shall I say resolved?—to be pleased ; but it could not be altogether due to this. The congregation was an immense one, the largest we had hitherto addressed, larger even than that which we had had at *Snizort;* and the sentiment of satisfaction was universal. As for Mr. Lillingston, who had never before heard our great pulpit orator, he was affected to his inmost soul. I saw the tears stream down his face. His handsome countenance shone as with a heavenly lustre. He told me afterwards that he had never listened to preaching like it ; I believed him ; I was sure he had not.

I said something to Dr. Candlish, afterwards, when we were alone, of the *liberty* he had evidently had in preaching. He admitted that he had felt very comfortable. He had, during the morning, he said, when roaming on the shore-beach, whilst I was preaching, gone over the subject thoroughly in his mind, and he knew that he was quite master of all the ideas.

" And why not adopt the same course always ?

Why be at any time fettered by *papers? O si sic semper!*"

"Bah! you don't understand. They would not have it."

"So much the greater loss for them," I said; "I wish some of the objectors had heard you to-day."

I have no doubt the effect of this visit to *Lochalsh* was good—very good. Mr. Lillingston's mind was made better disposed towards us in our various efforts as a Church, and in all our progress. He was made to feel, more than he had previously done, in spite of his prelatic proclivities, that the Free Church was a great power in the land, and that the movement was eminently of God. He had always been friendly, but it was on the general principle of favouring the *gospel* in *us*, without regard to our distinctive position. I think that, subsequent to this visit, there was more than this which animated him in the favour which he extended to our work.

With this day's services the THIRD WEEK of our tour was brought to a close; and here, consequently, the record of the THREE WEEKS terminates. But we have still to reach the end of our journey. *Concluding days*, therefore, fall to be added to what has already been written; and to the story of these days another chapter must be devoted—perhaps a long one.

CONCLUDING DAYS.

I.

ON Monday morning (18th August) Mr. M'Leod joined us at *Balmacara*. There he had always been, and till the end continued to be, a very special favourite. Mr. Lillingston had succeeded in producing in him a very decided conviction of the truth of his own pre-millennial personal advent beliefs. To Mr. M'Leod these beliefs became, as I knew, the occasion of much joy and comfort.

In course of the afternoon our party embarked once more on board the *Breadalbane*. Our destination was *Janetown*, near the head of *Lochcarron*, and our course lay from *Lochalsh*, through *Kyle Akin*, and northward for about twenty miles. At *Janetown* a conveyance was to meet us, by which we were to proceed on the following day to *Dingwall*, and thence to *Inverness*, whither the General Assembly of the Free Church was gathering from all quarters.

The day on which we entered on this, our last voyage for this time, was bright and promising;

the wind was strong enough, and sufficiently fair, to warrant the hope of comfortable progress.

We calculated much on the strong tide which was setting in the direction of our advance. Two or three hours, we felt assured, would see us arrived at our resting-place for the night.

We were disappointed. The breeze failed us. Towards sundown, not a breath stirred the surface, whilst the flood-tide ceased, and the ebb set in. We could expect to make no more progress for six hours to come, as the *Breadalbane* was not a steamship.

> " Down dropped the breeze, the sails dropped down,
>   'Twas sad as sad could be ;
>   And we did speak only to break
>   The silence of the sea !

> " Hour after hour, hour after hour,
>   We stuck, nor breath nor motion ;
>   As idle as a painted ship
>   Upon a painted ocean."—*Ancient Mariner.*

It was essential, however, that *we* should move on. We must needs reach *Janetown* some time that night, to be prepared for the journey before us for next day. There was but one alternative. We had the yacht's boat, not very commodious, but she was all that we could avail ourselves of in the circumstances. It was an arduous undertaking thus to pursue our journey. The distance to be accomplished was great; our motive power was weak; the cargo on board was heavy; and there were risks, of which I was more aware than any one in our small craft. To avoid the strength of the tide as much as possible, we pulled close in shore. This exposed us to a risk, of which I endeavoured to give due intimation both to the rowers and to our steersman, who was Dr. Candlish. I had been here before, on an occasion which I was quite willing to describe to my fellow voyagers. I had seen the bed of sunken rocks, which, I believed, we were approaching, which, if there were no run of tide, would be harmless to a rowing boat, but which, with such a run as we were now experiencing, I feared might prove dangerous. If we encountered the rocky bed, and had not depth enough above it to float us fairly over, in case the boat came broadside to, our condition might be perilous. The general opinion of those on board was that we were not so close inshore as to bring us into contact with the rocks, and that, if we were, we should have depth enough of water to float us comfortably over them.

I did feel anxiety—more, for a few minutes, on this occasion, than at any time during all our Highland tour. The boat carried Cæsar; she had a precious cargo ; and it did not prevent or allay my trouble, that no one seemed to care for the thing. I contented myself by urging on the oarsmen that, in case we did touch the rocks, they should not cease to pull, but rather pull the harder, to keep the boat's head in the stream, and by all means to prevent her turning round broadside to the current. The steersman was made to understand his duty likewise, and seemed a little amused at my carefulness.

We had not gone far, after this conversation on the probable, or possible, risk, till we felt our boat graze on the rock. The shadows of the evening were now gathering round us, and the first intimation of our presence on the rocky ground could only be in the form in which it thus unpleasantly came on us. We could *see* nothing. We pulled on ; again the boat's keel rubbed the bottom ; I cast a glance at Mr. Rory's face ; he was calm and undisturbed. Anything like panic might have proved disastrous ; there was none of that. A third time we came into contact with the rock, the tide rushing on ; this time, however, the collision was slight, showing that, in God's good providence, we were past the danger. We had got beyond the ledge over which we had held our course, and which existed, as I knew, only at this point. I felt very thankful then, as I always feel thankful now, when this incident occurs to my mind.

"How did you come to know so well about this rocky bed?" Dr Candlish asked. "Come, let us hear." Dr. M'Kellar expressed a similar request; and, although I declared it was not worth narrating, I told my story.

"I had come across from *Glenelg*, on one occasion, to pass a day with my kind friend at *Balmacara*. The weather was calm and enticing. We had had a long conversation on religious subjects. Unexpectedly he said to me, 'Have you ever seen *skate-fishing?*' 'Never,' I answered. The bell was rung. 'Send Allister here.' Allister, his faithful and much-esteemed servant, forthwith appeared. 'Allister, would not this be a fine afternoon for the skate at the bay, where we were lately?' 'There could not be better. The tide is flowing; we could get to the ground by half-flood; there is not a cloud in the sky, and the calm is perfect.'

"'Let the men get the boat ready; have out the spears with their tackle; and come yourself with us. I want to show the *minister* how to take skate.' I fancied there was a touch of humour in the way he referred to me; and I was sure he had something in store which he believed would either amuse or surprise me.

"We were soon on board the boat. The pull was a long one ; but with a strong tide, and able oarsmen, we made rapid progress, and soon came to the fishing-ground. It was a small bay, inshore, which, but for the darkness, we might now descry —at least the entrance to it. The ledge of seaward rocks over which we have passed lies outside the bay, and somewhat to the north-east of it. We were close on, if we did not pass over it, as we approached the fishing-ground. Mr. Lillingston spoke of the dangerous character of the ledge, and narrated several accidents to which it had given occasion. This impressed itself on my mind, and accounts for my anxiety this evening.

"The bay was shallow, with a sandy bottom of pure white. The sea was like glass, and the water was pellucid, clear as crystal. When our boat approached the bay, orders were given that the oars should be shipped, and that the boat should be allowed to float on the flood-tide, which would be sufficient to carry her quietly forward to the point we wished to reach. We were soon midway between the two sides of the tiny inlet, and perhaps a gunshot or more from the beautiful white beach in front. We floated on the surface, in perfect stillness, at the height, as we believed, judging by appearances, of from sixteen to thirty feet. The bottom, which was composed of white sand, looked very near, and was minutely visible. In entering the bay we suddenly glided upon this bright basin from a dark underground, occasioned, as I discovered on looking back through the water, by marine vegetation in its richest form, and on a scale such as I had never before witnessed. The appearance which it assumed was that of a lofty bank, adown which were visible shady groves, furnished to excess with the foliage peculiar to the sea, floating and waving gracefully, as the mass yielded to the varied influences of the moving tide. 'What a gorgeous retreat,' I exclaimed, 'is provided here for the protection and enjoyment of its many and varied occupants ! How great is the goodness of the faithful Creator, and how perfect is his wisdom !'

" 'O Lord, how wonderful are thy works ! in wisdom hast thou made them all : the earth is full of thy riches ; so is this great and wide sea.' *

"Turning from the contemplation of this submarine grove, and casting my eyes to the other portion of the picture spread out for our admiration, what an *aquarium* did I behold ! Near the

* Psalm civ. 24, 25.

O

surface a vast shoal of the smaller tribes of fish
disported themselves, apparently in the enjoyment
of perfect animal happiness ; lower down were
seen fish of a larger size, of many descriptions ;
lowest of all were the flat fish, including flounders,
urbot, and our gam e, the skate — those inter-
mingled with specimens of the lobster and crab
tribes of every class, which floated or swam
or crept along the smooth sandy bottom.   It
was most interesting to watch the creatures
issuing from what appeared to be their hiding
or dwelling places in the darksome groves, which
seemed to my eyes to form so romantic a
seclusion for them.   Especially was it so to watch
the huge, broad-backed, bright-eyed forms for
which we were on the look-out.   There was great
rapidity and stealthiness in their movements.
One object with them, very decidedly, was not to be
perceived.   As they appeared through the medium
of the water, their colour differed but little from
that of the sandy bottom, so that it required much
quickness of eye to follow their rapid motion
as they skimmed along.   Especially difficult was
it to detect them when concealed in the soft
powdery deposit which, with great adroitness and
the least possible disturbance, they covered themselves with, and quietly nestled in.   But for the

bright eyes, which could. not with safety be covered or concealed, no power of human vision could have perceived them. The eyes once perceived, it was not difficult, aided by the imagination and the slight quivering of the fins in the moving waters, to trace the outline of the body.

"As our boat floated on the surface, in deep silence, we beheld a large specimen come and settle itself so close to us, that there could be no doubt it would soon be within reach of our instruments of death. Another and another, as if following the lead of the first, gathered under, or near to, the shadow created by our boat. All on board showed some excitement, and as there was one spear provided for each, every man seized his weapon. It was a trident, with formidable prongs, well barbed. The prongs were about eight inches long, and the barbs were such as to make the escape of the prey, if once pierced, impossible. The shaft was long, generally about twenty feet, and was furnished with a hard strong cord, fastened carefully to its upper extremity.

"'You had better see me do it first,' Mr. Lillingston whispered to me, as he noticed me, like the others, preparing for action. 'It is not quite an easy thing to send the spear through the water direct to the prey. The effect of the refraction-is such as greatly to deceive the inexperienced sportsman.'

"I was happy to be instructed by such a master in what could not certainly, in the present instance, be described as the *gentle* art. The boatmen awaited his instructions as it became them.

"He handled the long-shafted spear very gently and very quietly, scarcely creating a ripple on the surface as it passed through the water. Down and down it slowly went—now no longer a straight pole, but the portion under the surface appearing at an angle so great to the portion still in the air, that I could not believe it possible the prongs could be guided straight to the fish. To my apprehension the weapon was not, by a foot or two, approaching the spot where I was able easily to trace the outline of the poor victim, so soon to experience that its fate was but too surely settled. The sharp points proceeded slowly but steadily towards the bottom. It was impossible to tell by the eye how near or how far from it they were. My eyes followed the instrument with a strange sort of interest. In a moment, the sportsman raised his right hand to the upper extremity of the shaft, directing it with his left, and grasping it firmly in perfect quietness. Then there was a sudden thrust given with all the vigour of an

athlete. This done, he sat back with great cool-
ness, holding in his hand the cord, several feet of
which had followed the spear when plunged into
the deep. A cloud of powdery sand obscured our
vision of the bottom, and presently the spear-
shaft was seen to ascend slowly in a slanting
direction to the surface. It rose gradually with a
strange tremulousness, moving a little, sometimes
to the one hand, sometimes to the other. An un-
seen power was affecting it. As the agitated sand
began to subside, and the medium of vision became clear, the cause was made palpable. A skate
of large dimensions, transfixed through the very
centre of its body, was seen, in spite of its
struggles and the flapping of its huge fins, to be
raised by the buoyant power of the spear-shaft
closer and closer to the surface. The cord was
employed to draw the shaft towards our boat, and
the fishing process was soon completed by this late
inhabitant of the umbrageous marine grottoes, over
which he had but a little ago passed, being made
the spoil of the lords of creation, to whom power
has been given, from the source of all authority,
'over the fish of the sea,' as well as over the
other creatures made 'to be taken and destroyed.'

" The work of destruction went on rapidly. The
boatmen declared they had never seen such a shoal

of skate before. It was suggested that the number might have been quite as great on other occasions, although the opportunity of *seeing* them might not have been so good. This was admitted. The slaughter now was appalling; but all my efforts to kill my fish failed. I could not calculate correctly the necessary allowance for the apparent angle created by the refraction of the water. But I really congratulated myself afterwards on my want of success, when I beheld the staring bloodshot eyes of the butchered throng, as they lay in the boat—such a multitude in their blood—in death, or in their dying moments, seeming as if they cast looks of reproach or vindictiveness at their unfeeling and too successful pursuers. Our cargo was soon complete; it could not be said that we returned 'clean.' Catching the first of ebb, the pull to *Balmacara* was soon over. On reaching the shore, orders were given for the disposal of our booty, all the poor who were to have a share being distinctly named by the leader of our expedition.

"On more than on one occasion, it appeared strange to me that a man of such gentleness and such tenderness of disposition as Mr. Lillingston, should seem to care so little for inflicting death on the inferior creation. I accounted for it by remembering that, from early life, he must have been acquainted with the field sports to which the English aristocracy devote themselves. In the Highlands he was no enthusiast in such sports. Though his property abounded in red deer, I never heard of his going a deer-stalking, or of his joining any of his aristocratic compatriots in Ross-shire in such pursuits, or almost in any matters in which they were fond of distinguishing themselves. Yet there can be no doubt that he was an expert in every exercise which required agility, strength, and skill. He might have gained the highest reputation, had he sought it, in that way. He had been taught, however, to delight himself with higher things—a truth not inconsistent with his enjoying occasionally such a *battue* as we had this day indulged in. On the way home, with scarcely an observation upon it, he shot down—it might be only to discharge his double-barrel—some of the hungry sea-fowl which the sight or the savour of our cargo attracted towards and around us."

II.

This story, though here given continuously, was often interrupted by my companions asking many questions, and making many demands for explanation and additional information—all of which I rejoiced to give.

Our progress was slow; but still we made progress. The night was on us; but it was not dark; and we ran no risk of collisions. After we had passed the ferry which divides the *Lochcarron* region from *Lochalsh,* we advanced at better speed; but it was long past midnight ere, with aching bones and benumbed frames, we set foot on the slippery, seaweed-covered, low-water shore, skirting the small village of *Janetown.* We had passed a day of some adventure, and we felt thankful that our journey was done. The lights in the inn showed that we were expected. The inmates there knew too well the uncertainties connected with sea travelling, and could calculate too well the effects of adverse tides, to be surprised that we had not put in appearance at a somewhat earlier hour. A good fire blazed in the grate of the "big room;" the table was covered, ready for our refreshment; the sight of which, with the change from the cold sea air to the comfortable temperature within, made us both thankful and cheerful.

My first anxiety, after our safe arrival, was to ascertain whether the conveyance which was, next day, to carry us to *Dingwall,* had arrived. I soon learned that a two-horse chaise, of good capacity, had arrived in course of the evening, and would be ready for us at any hour we chose next morning.

It was enough; there was to be no disappointment in this respect; and there was to be no Dr. Lee to appear to displace or to supersede us.

A comfortable sleep, and a hearty breakfast at an early hour, prepared us for the journey of next day. It must needs be arduous, for the way was long. The road from *Janetown* to *Dingwall* runs through more than one of the most magnificent straths in the Highlands—a road far from mountainous; indeed, all but level throughout, the exception being a portion towards the *Dingwall* termination. In modern times a railway has traced its course. In 1845 no imagination had conceived the possibility of such a phenomenon.

The carriage was well filled, when Dr. M'Kellar, Mr. M'Leod, Dr. Candlish, and I, took possession. The day was favourable; the roads were smooth; the horses fresh. Moreover, we were about to complete our tour. Another day, and we expected to arrive at the grand *rendezvous*, towards which hundreds of the friends of our Church were wending their way, from every point of the compass.

As we got into the carriage, looking down the loch, over whose surface we had been conveyed on the previous night, we saw the white sails of the BREADALBANE, far down, brightly reflecting the morning sun. She had no wind, and appeared to be as motionless as she was when we abandoned her. The tide had, during the night, floated her on, through the ferry, up the loch, into her present position; where, no doubt, she would remain, until the returning tide and a favouring wind carried her again into the open sea. She was soon lost to our view. As we proceeded on our journey, we saw her no more; but we ever cherished happy recollections of our pleasant voyage in her, and of the urbanity, kindness, and sailor manliness of her commander, Captain M'Ewen.

Whilst partaking of breakfast in the "big room" at *Janetown*, I chanced to say, "Well, I have seen some scenes here which were of interest to me at the time; especially on the first occasion on which I looked on these walls with their grotesque furnishings."

"Ah, you must let us hear about that when we get upon the road; I have heard that you had a battle to fight to make good your footing in Glenelg," Dr. Candlish said.

"I am afraid I weary you with my recitals," I replied; "but when one comes upon localities which remind him of the past, he cannot avoid speaking of events which they recall—at least so it is with me—my infirmity perhaps, but happy when I have listeners good-natured enough to bear with me."

III.

" Early in the summer of 1830, I was presented
by Lord Glenelg (the Right Hon. Charles Grant)
to the parish of Glenelg, in the estate from which
he took his title. I was at the time in the ninth
year of my ministry, and settled in the parish of
Kilbrandon. His lordship being desirous of securing a minister for Glenelg holding views on
religious questions in harmony with his own, he
was directed to me by friends in Edinburgh,
whom he consulted. It was somewhat of a surprise to receive from this good man a letter
narrating what he had done, describing the importance of the parish in his gift as patron, his
desire to have it supplied satisfactorily, and pre-
senting for my consideration several inducements
for accepting the presentation which he was
prepared to issue in my favour, on my agreeing to
accept. I had difficulties ; the chief being the
succession to *Kilbrandon.* This leading difficulty
having been removed by the probability, almost
certainty—God favouring—of my cousin, Mr., now
Dr. Elder of Rothesay, being appointed to *Kilbrandon,* I agreed to accept the presentation to
Glenelg. My cousin did become my successor in
the derelict parish—a comfort to me, and, as it
proved, a blessing to many.

" The presentation to Glenelg was lodged with
the Moderator of the Presbytery of Lochcarron in
good, that is within the statutory, time, though
somewhat late. On this ground it could not be
objected to, although some expectation was entertained that it might. Dr. Ross, of Lochbroom—a
man well known in his time—was Moderator on
this occasion. The relative papers were duly
lodged, along with the presentation. That there
might be no mistake, a legal official carried all
the documents *in propriâ personâ* from *Inverness*
to the manse of Lochbroom, and before witnesses
deposited them in the hands of the dignified head,
pro tempore, of the Presbytery.

" The rejection of my presentation, however, was
a foregone conclusion. Dr. Ross discovered a
defect that, to him, appeared irremediable. Of the
six months within which the patron might present, there remained, when the presentation was
placed in his hands, but a few hours. A new
presentation and new relative documents could not,
by any stratagem or any effort, be in that time provided ; the case was a clear one. *Jure devoluto*,
the Presbytery, and as representing that body, he,
for this *vice*, was to be patron of the lucrative, and
most desirable parish of Glenelg !

" A meeting of Presbytery was summoned to be

held at *Janetown* on a given day. It was a full meeting—a meeting big with thoughts of the important transaction that was then to be consummated. The presentation in my favour, and the other papers connected with it, were laid on the table. All my documents were full and correct; so was the patron's, with one exception. He had not qualified to Government—the presentee had; the certificate of his having done so, with his letter of acceptance, was all right, but the patron had not qualified to Government; no evidence was before the court to show that *he* had! It was unanimously found that the presentation could not be sustained—it must be set aside. Moreover, the Presbytery, looking to the circumstances of the parish, and the importance of having it without delay supplied with a minister, resolved to proceed to exercise their privilege, in the circumstances, of appointing a minister. They did so. A son of the late minister was named as a suitable successor. He was a young probationer of amiable character, and it looked a generous and kind thing to the family of which he was a member, that he should be selected. The appointment was made and regularly recorded; the usual procedure with a view to the settlement being at the same time arranged. Intimation of what had thus been done was ordered to be made officially by the clerk to both the Patron and his Presentee. The transaction was complete; there were congratulations on all hands; the new presentee was called in, and he declared his acceptance.

" On a day not long after this I received by post, at *Kilbrandon*, the communication which the clerk had been instructed to make to me.

"I, too, like my rival presentee, had been receiving congratulations; and, in our manse, we had been forecasting the future—resolving in our minds on arrangements which would be required, and which might be warranted by the change in our circumstances, as well as in our new place of abode. We felt it to be an untoward event; it gave us an unpleasant shock, but we felt we could survive it. The rumour that I was to leave *Kilbrandon* had created no small excitement there, and had called forth such an amount of affectionate feeling, as well as of effort in the direction of taking steps to prevent my removal, that we had relentings of heart in looking forward to that event.

" The matter had not taken end, however. Not many days after receipt of the letter from the clerk of the Presbytery of *Lochcarron*, a large packet, addressed to me, was delivered at the manse. On opening it, my eye caught the title of a printed document folded in lawyer-like form, very ominous of evil to look at. It was the copy of a summons of interdict, concluding for damages, directed against the Moderator and other members of the Presbytery of *Lochcarron*, and, in most energetic terms, describing their 'outrageous' conduct in interfering with the legal rights of the Patron of the parish of Glenelg, Inverness-shire, contrary to law, etc. etc. The document had been drawn by Lord Glenelg's Edinburgh agent, the late Mr. Hugh M'Queen, a man considered, in his day, to be one of the ablest agents ever entitled to append W.S. to his name. He had drawn the presentation, and had arranged the details of all the relative papers. The Inverness agent, the late Sheriff-substitute Edwards, had advised that Lord Glenelg's qualification to Government should form one of these papers; but Mr. M'Queen, who had carefully studied the terms of the statute with a view to the case, declared that this was not required.

" The bill presented by him to the Court of Session embodied a most masterly argument for the patron, and a withering exposure of the Presbytery's conduct. He proved that, under the circumstances, the certificate of Lord Glenelg's qualification was not essential, he being a member of the Government, and having often qualified; but particularly, he proved, by the terms of the statute, that, even should the want of the certificate in question be found to be an objection fatal to the validity of the presentation, and should that document be set aside, and my nomination be cancelled thereby, the right to present did not fall to the Presbytery but to the Crown. That the Court perceived the force of the argument, was evident by a Bill of interdict and suspension being at once passed.

" A private letter to me, inclosed in the packet, announced that the case would speedily be called in Court ; and instructed me to disregard overtures which might be made by the Presbytery—on all the members of which the interdict had been served —or by any other party. A letter from Sheriff Edwards, a day or two later, informed me that the serving of the interdict had created great dismay throughout the bounds of the Presbytery of Loch-carron, some of the members of which had called on him ; that a meeting of the body was forthwith to be summoned, of which he would give me notice in case I did not otherwise hear of it ; and, as it might be proper, if not necessary, that I should attend on the occasion, I should hold myself ready to undertake the journey to *Janetown*, the seat of Presbytery, when the day of meeting came to be known.

"I made up my mind, after much consideration, to be guided by my patron's agents, and I prepared, accordingly, for a journey to the *north*—a region which I had never previously visited.

"No long time elapsed until a fresh communication from Inverness informed me that a meeting of the peccant Presbytery had been summoned, to be held, at their usual seat, on the 14th of July, in the matter of the presentation to *Glenelg*, and advised that I should by all means appear there. I was at the same time invited to come to *Inverness* on my way, where I should be furnished with such instructions as I might require, or as might be useful in guiding my course.

"The journey was long, and one which I should not have undertaken except for the special circumstances which seemed to demand it, as well as the awkward position in which my patron was placed by the hostility of the Presbytery.

"My travels included *Oban, Fort-William*, the *Caledonian Canal, Inverness, Dingwall*, and thence through *Strathconon* to *Janetown*. I tarried a few hours at *Inverness* to receive instructions there. A fixed determination, I found, prevailed to resist the Presbytery. At the same time, there was a strong desire expressed to me, that, if I possibly could effect it, the Presbytery should be got to rescind their past proceedings, to sustain my presentation, and proceed with my settlement. I was authorised, in case I saw them inclined so to act, or in case I could prevail with them to that effect, to hold out the prospect that no further proceedings would be taken against them in the courts of law. I was empowered, besides, to take with me from *Dingwall* a law-agent, to whom I had, from Mr. Edwards, a letter of instructions to assist, in case any difficulties of a legal kind might arise.

" It was Friday when I arrived at *Inverness.* Late that night I proceeded by mail to *Invergordon* and *Rosskeen*, there to visit my much-esteemed and early friend, Mr. Carment. On the Sabbath I preached in his huge church to a most interesting congregation. On my way, I likewise visited Mr. Donald Fraser, then minister of Kirkhill, the eminent predecessor and father of the present much respected Free Church minister there. I should rejoice to have an opportunity of recording all I know of Mr. Donald Fraser, as well as of Mr. Carment. At the manse of the former I met with a member of the Presbytery, whose meeting I was on my way to attend. He was a relation of the minister of Kirkhill, and held himself to be innocent of the mischief which his brethren had committed in the case of my presentation. Indeed, he affected greatly to deplore it, and expressed himself most ready to do what he could to remedy it. The interdict had been served on him, and had produced a most salutary effect. This was so far encouraging to me, in view of the object of my journey. Mr. Fraser entered frankly into the whole question, and gave me sound counsel as to the mode in which I should deal with the Presbytery. He anticipated, however, very determined resistance, and, notwithstanding the terrors of the law courts, a sure case for the Assembly.

"I travelled by a one-horse two-wheeled open conveyance, which I had hired at *Inverness*. For the first two stages my way lay through a rich and most charming country ; thereafter through a series of enchanting glens and straths. The weather, to crown all, was superb, and the country was quite new to me.

" Previous to this visit to the north, I had had the impression that the further one proceeded in that direction from the central counties, the more into the wilderness and the " Highlands" proper. But, so far from this, I found in the country around *Inverness* and *Dingwall* a highly cultivated and a magnificently rich-wooded land, abounding with country residences, not surpassed in magnitude and beauty by any even in the neighbourhood of *Edinburgh,* or belonging to our first nobility. On leaving that district behind, as I advanced in my journey into the western portions of Ross-shire, where the county again marches with Inverness-shire, I passed over roads level and smooth, running through valleys, the tops of the mountains on each side seeming to pierce the clouds—a country, however, almost without inhabitants, and occupied only by the simple sheep and the timid deer.

"Late in the evening I arrived at *Achnasheen* (the stage to which we are now advancing), having performed a journey of nearly fifty miles, and having still some twenty miles to travel ere I should reach *Janetown.* Next day at twelve it behoved the reverend court to meet, so that I had abundant time to reach the scene of action by the hour of call.

"There had been a sheep-shearing ('clipping') at *Achnasheen.* Scores of shepherd-dogs lay about the doors and outhouses of the small thatched inn at which we alighted, and where we were to make our abode for the. night. The shepherds were not quite so numerous as their dogs, but they *were* numerous, being congregated from all parts of the district, for mutual aid, as is usual on such occasions ;—tall, strong, active-looking men, dressed in the short blue plaiding jacket of the country, and the kilt in every variety of colour. The labour of the day was past; they were all,—men and dogs—retiring to rest; every corner of the inn was in their possession, except the double-bedded room, which was to serve my companions and myself as dining-room, drawing-room, and sleeping apartment. The former were the patron's lawyer —a grim-looking man, to whose locomotion a large crutch, which he used with great dexterity, was necessary—and his clerk; both had joined me at Dingwall. As they travelled in a separate conveyance, we looked formidable, and were all the more so that our legal friend was a sort of factor or land-agent on the property on which our inn for the night was situated.

"In due time we went to bed, but not to sleep. The possession and sure custody of his dog, on the eve of a 'gathering,' is to a shepherd a very important consideration. Without him he is then helpless. On the present occasion, the whole tribe of shepherds assembled was to have *day second* of their sheep-shearing, and the men required, accordingly, to be off by early dawn to the mountains, for a fresh relay of the woolly denizens, for subjection to an operation which to them in hot weather must surely be enjoyable. Every man had

his brace, or more, of dogs, either sharing his
bed, such as it might be, or reposing near his
person,—the object being to prevent wandering
against the time of need. The apartment above
ours was densely occupied. It had no carpet, of
course, neither had it any 'deafening;' the bare
thin boards of the floor were all that separated it
from us. We were in the closest possible prox-
imity with its inhabitants of both kinds, short of
being actually within the same enclosure. The
snoring of the men soon began, and was very
startling ; but what shall I say of their canine bed-
fellows ? They did not snore, but there was an occasional sound of snarling, with evident challenges
to battle. This was not the worst. When such
tumult ceased, and it never went very far, we were
every two or three minutes roused by RAPPING
overhead of the most nervous and energetic character. One after the other of the poor dogs, and
sometimes several together, exerted themselves
to get quit of the sheep-vermin that had fastened
in their skin, or of some other annoyance ; and,
scratching themselves vehemently with this view,
they beat rapidly with their elbows the wooden
flooring, causing hideous noise. So far as sleep
was concerned, our case was hopeless.

" At length, about three o'clock in the morning,

day broke, when, in less than ten minutes, as it
appeared to me, from the moment of the first
shout, commanding departure to the 'Hill,' all
our tormentors were gone. For a little I heard
the confused noise—loud whistling to the dogs,
their names hallooed, responsive barking on their
part, and the respective routes of men and dogs
energetically announced, as they took their leave
of the inn ; after which a most grateful stillness
supervened, when I fell into a profound slumber—
a slumber from which I awoke only to be in time
for the journey to *Janetown*, to keep tryst with the
Presbytery of Lochcarron. Of this incident I
have a very vivid recollection.

"We made it our study to present ourselves at
the Presbytery seat in good time. Some ten minutes
after twelve o'clock we arrived at the inn where
the meetings were always held, expecting to find
the brethren in full session. The *room* was vacant,
although manifestly prepared for the expected
clerical assemblage. There was not the slightest
indication of the arrival of any of the members of
the Court. They were looked for, we ascertained,
but when they might make appearance no con-
jecture could be formed. No one with whom
we came in contact seemed to be surprised at
this. I was ; and not surprised only, but annoyed

also, seeing I was set on having my business concluded, and getting back to the dormitory of the preceding night, on my way home, comfortless though that dormitory had been. But patience required to be exercised, considering that I was in the wilds of Ross-shire, and within the bounds of a very primitive Presbytery.

"About two o'clock, as I was seated in the large apartment, where we this morning breakfasted, waiting for the *meeting*, there walked in two very unique figures—ministers, unquestionably—but of a cast new to me, and, unhappily, suggesting something of the ludicrous. The one was, I had no doubt, the acknowledged *primus* of the other.

"He was a man of medium height, and of slight figure, in age approaching, if he had not attained, *sixty* years. His manner was frank and brusque. His eyes—one of them protruding more than the other—were dark—of the African hue, the ball, as well as the iris—the entire eye of a disagreeable yellow colour. He was the minister of the parish, and the successor of the celebrated Mr. Lachlan M'Kenzie of Lochcarron. He was a M'Kenzie as well, though of a different type, and well known over all the Northern Highlands by the sobriquet of "Potato John." The clan was so numerous that individuals of the same name had to be distinguished by some distinctive sobriquet. The present worthy received his distinctive appellation from the following incident, which, as it was at the time made public in the Church courts, there can be no impropriety in narrating.

"In his youth, and during all his life, he was noted for his *practical jokes*. Travelling home on one occasion from the University of Aberdeen, at the close of the session, on foot, with some other Ross-shire students of divinity, the party stopped at an inn by the way for dinner. The most advanced of them was the late Mr. M'Gillivray of Lairg, Sutherlandshire; a man even in youth distinguished for his piety. As on the occasion of other halts by the way, Mr. M'Gillivray presided, and proceeded to 'ask the blessing.' Whilst so engaged, his eyes firmly closed, his manner earnest, the palm of his hand held open, moving gently to and fro, whilst his elbow rested on the table, M'Kenzie, hungry for his dinner, thinking the *grace* by much too long, and eager to get at the potatoes, which were steaming hot, as they had just come from the pot to the table, resolved to bring the service to an abrupt close. In pursuance of this object, he lifted a potato from among the hottest in the dish, placed it rapidly in the open

palm of the chaplain, and with all his strength,
using both his hands, shut Mr. M'Gillivray's fingers
close down upon the potato, so as to burn him
severely. Summary punishment was about to be
inflicted on the culprit, but, by his superior agility,
he escaped. I had often heard the story, but I
had never before seen the hero of it.

"The other figure who accompanied him looked
to me very much like what we call a HALFLING.
He was considerably older than M'Kenzie—distinguished by a large head and massive features,
the hair of his head being cropped close to the
skull, for a reason of which I was not allowed to
be for any time ignorant. He was a M'RAE, and
rejoicing in the *Christian* name of *Rory*. He was
a schoolmaster, and had always been so ; having
at intervals, however, attended college at Aberdeen, he ultimately obtained license as a preacher.
In that capacity he continued for many years
doing duty as a missionary on the Royal Bounty
Scheme, in addition to his teaching. When the
Parliamentary Churches were erected in the Highlands, he became, by the influence of the proprietor
of Applecross, minister of the new charge of *Shiel-
daig*. Subsequently, on the death of Mr. M'Queen,
the much-esteemed minister of the parish of
Applecross, he was, through the same influence,

promoted to the incumbency of that charge. The voice of the people—*their* views and desires—had in those days no place in the settlement of their pastors, so that the appointment was not reclaimed against.

"The vainglory of this poor specimen of the clerical order was ridiculous. His friend, who introduced him to me, never failed to make a *butt* of him. He had persuaded him that he was quite the equal of *Cicero* in his knowledge of the Latin tongue, and in the beauty of his Latin composition. He proved it by comparing the shape of his head, and the contour of his countenance, with a stucco bust of the great Roman orator, which poor M'Rae had somewhere picked up, and which he highly prized. Believing this nonsense, the poor man had his hair regularly polled, that he might be held in admiration of all for his resemblance to the distinguished Roman.

"Neither of these men would be worthy of the notice I have taken of them, but for one circumstance. On the day of our great Disruption, when Dr. Welsh had finished the reading of the famous Protest, thrown it down on the table, taken up his hat, and moved away from the Moderator's chair in St. Andrew's church, followed by Dr. Chalmers, Dr. Cunningham, Dr. Candlish, and our other magnates, and when the Lord Commissioner, Lord Bute, appalled at what he saw taking place, tried to hide his head under the table before which he sat—the Lord Advocate (late Lord Colonsay), pale with emotion, advising him to retire, that he might not longer witness what was in progress (which he did), every man at the time holding his breath, affected by the solemnity of the scene,—then it was that two ministers, known apparently to no one, with the most perfect *nonchalance*, and expressing in their sneering countenances contempt for what was going on, were seen to pass over from the *Moderate* side of the house, and, in view of the assembled and overawed multitude, to plant themselves in the seats which had just been vacated by the great men I have named. These two ministers were the men whom I have just described. Few who at the time read the notice recorded by Hugh Miller in the *Witness* newspaper of this event, will forget his graphic description, or his severe animadversions—animadversions, however, which could not have had the slightest effect on the men against whom they were directed.

"After some general conversation, I said, 'I expected to meet the Presbytery here to-day at the hour usual on such occasions.'

"'You must know that the distances here for

members to travel are very great,' was the reply. Mr. JOHN has to come all the way from the head of *Loch Duich.* He usually sails, as he has a small yacht. It is a long sail. He will likely embark Mr. HECTOR at Lochalsh as he passes; that will detain him. Besides, the wind has not been good to-day, and I think the tide has not been favourable.' (Mr. JAMES was with us.)

" ' When do you expect him and his friend to arrive ?'

" Oh, some time in course of the evening. He might make the journey by land, round the head of *Loch Duich,* but that route would be very fatiguing. Then Dr. Ross requires two days to make the journey from his manse at *Lochbroom* to the seat of Presbytery; last night he must have been at *Garve*—no farther. He cannot be here before nightfall.'

" ' You will surely constitute and do your business, at any rate, before the day is done ?'

" ' We usually arrange to constitute on the day appointed for our meeting—we seldom do more; the business follows on the succeeding day; and, for the most part, but not always, we conclude on the second day; but just as frequently not till the third day.'

" Here, to be sure, was a pretty prospect for me,

running over, as I was, with impatience. I secretly persuaded myself, however, that, if I lived to become a member of the Court, I would try to produce a reform in this particular. Meanwhile, I felt my part was to submit and be content.

" ' We always dine before we enter on business, and to-day, as many of us as may appear will dine at *four* o'clock. You and your friends will of course join us ?' To this we assented.

" Our dinner was all but concluded, when the two members who had been expected to come by sea entered the room. I scanned their appearance with interest and some anxiety. The one was a tall vigorous-looking man—about my own age as I reckoned—then very little over *thirty*, of high well-developed forehead, expressive of intellect, blue eyes, and of quiet demeanour. The other was a man older considerably, of less than the middle size, by no means imposing in his aspect, and by no means of air or bearing indicative of superiority of any kind—carelessly dressed, and of awkward gait, evidently arising from some infirmity in one of his limbs. Both seemed to be ambitious, judging by various indications, of being counted boatmen or yachtsmen, as if eminence in that department was in their estimation eminence worth possessing, or ought to be considered so by all men. The former was 'Mr. JOHN,' the latter 'Mr. HECTOR.' My first impressions of both were favourable. I conceived that they were men who could understand what was reasonable, and who would be more apt to act under the influence of a calm understanding than of unreasoning passion in any form. My subsequent experience confirmed the accuracy of my first impressions. I always respected ' Mr. John ' as a practical, strong-headed, though not always judicious, brother. I came to entertain genuine esteem and regard for 'Mr. Hector.' He was a man of honesty and upright-ness according to his light—less a party man than any *Moderate* minister I ever knew—always kind, and even affectionate, not being accessible to offence on any point, unless it was in the matter of the antiquity of all that was Highland, the superior excellence of the Gaelic tongue as com-pared with all other languages, and the equality of *Ossianic* poetry to *Homeric*. *Fingal*, he always maintained, was quite on a par with the *Iliad*. He never fairly forgave me for producing on one occasion, as the result of a challenge on his part, a description of his own person and character, in inflated Ossianic Gaelic, all the terms of which were borrowed—he not knowing it—from the so-called Celtic epic, which had been, in the name of

Ossian, published under the auspices of the HIGH-
LAND SOCIETY of *Scotland.* I need scarcely add
that neither of these clergymen was ever popular
as a *preacher,* though they were both held in much
esteem for their general respectability and bene-.
volence.

· " Our conversation, after dinner, turned on the
matter which had brought me at this time among
them. A letter which had come from Dr. Ross
before I left home, had raised in my mind a suspi-·
cion that he really was the author of all the mischief connected with the rejection of my presentation. This came out clearly now, and all the more
that Dr. Ross put in no appearance at this meeting. It was not the first time, they were ready to
tell me, he had led them on the ice and left them
there. We soon came to an understanding. They
were prepared to cancel all their proceedings in
the case, to sustain my presentation, and to proceed
with my settlement. They desired, naturally, to
have some guarantee for their being released from
the terrors of the law courts. In that matter I
went as far as I was warranted to do by the instructions which had been given me at *Inverness.*
I could do no more. They were satisfied. Practically the whole affair was settled before we retired
to rest. The Presbytery was constituted, my ap-

pearance there was minuted, as well as the object I had in view in making appearance as a party,—after which the Court adjourned. Next day they resumed, when the formalities were regularly gone through,—all arrangements being appointed for my settlement in Glenelg in the month of September, an event which accordingly took place. The lawyer was not required. It was of much importance for my future usefulness in this region, that there should be an amicable termination of the awkward mistake into which they had been led. Lord Glenelg was much impressed with this, and desired, at whatever cost, to accomplish it.

"I may say that, for the nine years during which I was connected with this Presbytery, my communications with all its members—if I may except Dr. Ross—were pleasant. I did what I could to help in the business of the Court. They all came to have confidence in me, and I laboured not to abuse that confidence. I preached in their parishes as I had opportunity, and I believe that, throughout the entire, wide-spread district to which I thus had access, evangelical truth came to be highly valued and to be earnestly sought after. Within two years of my becoming a member of Presbytery, the representative elder to the Assembly, one of the highest of the *Moderate* laymen there, a W.S. of considerable name, was unseated. In his place we chose, in the first instance, Dr. Welsh; and, when he was compelled to resign on account of his necessary absence from Scotland, we elected as his successor Mr. Alexander Dunlop, who continued to be our representative in the Free, as he had been in the Established Church Assembly, with what advantage to our church and country we all know.*

"Our business completed at *Janetown*, I returned with all speed to *Inverness*, were I had the happiness of being introduced to my patron, Lord Glenelg, to whom I narrated the success which had attended my journey to the west, much to his joy and satisfaction. Thereafter I soon found my way home to Kilbrandon."

This narrative, as in other cases, was by no means allowed to be continuous. Various remarks were made on the circumstances as I stated them.

---

* It does not always happen that a *name* can be held as security for the practice of virtues which it is intended or understood to represent. Melancholy instances of the contrary sometimes occur. I have lived to see a Presbytery of Lochcarron (FREE (?)) supersede (stupidly, not to use a harsher term) Mr. Murray Dunlop and Mr. Brown Douglas, as their Assembly representatives, for others whom, to spare them, I shall not name. I cannot say, taking them all in all, that I could prefer to the Presbytery of 1830, ESTABLISHED, the Presbytery of 1870, FREE.

One thing we all expressed, and that was thankfulness for our deliverance as a Church from *patronage*. At the time I was speaking of, everything depended upon the action of the patron. His sense of what was right and proper was supreme, no interference of any kind being permitted to overrule his decision. Even when the patron was a man such as Lord Glenelg, who in many respects was better qualified than the people to choose their pastor, and who discharged this duty with the most conscientious regard for their spiritual well-being, we felt that the relation in which he stood to them was unnatural, unscriptural, and dangerous.

"I say, Beith, did I not once advise you to write down your recollections of men and events in your early experience?" Dr. Candlish said to me.

"You did," I answered; "and you encouraged me by saying that the time would come when what I wrote might be valuable as illustrating the condition of the church and of society in my days."

"And have you been doing what I then recommended?"

"I have. Your advice was that I should so employ, faithfully, *one hour* in the week, permitting nothing to interfere with it; and you said if I did I would be surprised how matter would accumulate on my hands. Before you suggested this, I had done something in the direction which you had kindly indicated. I did more, afterwards, and it is my purpose to continue the practice. If I had not had a record of the things with which I have been either entertaining or plaguing you now, I could not have so easily narrated them. One evil, if I may so call it, arises from this—namely, that, when I come on the scenes, and when I meet with persons who have formed the subjects of my notes, I cannot, as I have already told you, help talking of them, if those who are with me are good-natured enough to listen patiently to my talk." I was encouraged on all hands.

We had had a long day's journey when we arrived at Dingwall. We had visited *Achnasheen* by the way, where I pointed out my dormitory of fifteen years before. There were changes, but the parlour, with its deal floor overhead, was still there, and much as it was. Sportsmen from England had given Achnasheen a celebrity which in 1830 did not attach to it. One advantage we experienced from this change was our having *grouse* and other game, in every variety of cooking, served up to us for dinner, on this our journey eastward.

At *Dingwall* we rested for the night. Next day was to be the last of the concluding days of our

tour. Although happy that the toil of travel was
drawing to a close, I looked forward with much
regret to the prospect of parting with my very
agreeable fellow-travellers, and particularly with
Dr. Candlish, who had been my close companion
for more than THREE WEEKS.

IV.

In the preceding account of our TOUR, I have
scarcely referred at all to the religious services of
various kinds, which engaged us during the time
it lasted. I think I may say truly that our hearts
were set on doing good as our Master might bless
us. I can testify for Dr. Candlish, that I never
witnessed, on his part, greater earnestness and
solemnity in all that he engaged in. ·Sometimes
deep impressions seemed to be produced in the
minds of his hearers by his most effective services.
We could but hope, as we prayed, and as we
believed, that fruit might in due time appear.
For myself, I can only say that I experienced
special delight in returning for a season to my
old work of preaching and speaking in the
vernacular of the country. During nineteen
years previous to my settlement at Stirling, I had
preached chiefly in the Gaelic tongue. It was impossible, consequently, that I could ever lose the
use of it entirely. A man who *can* preach in

Gaelic with ease will never prefer the other. If the choice be left to him, he will certainly betake himself to the mountain tongue. I do not say the matter was left to my *choice* on the occasion of this excursion. We were all under orders. But that the choice had been so made for me, added much to my enjoyment.

I find that I preached in all about twenty times in course of our journey, besides taking part in other services, and sharing in the consultations touching matters which claimed our attention at every step: the correspondence was also wholly in my hands.

Dr. Candlish, though he did not *preach* quite so frequently as I did, gave addresses of various kinds, and, upon the whole, carried a heavier burden of work and effort than I did. No man could do it more gracefully. I often thought with myself what a noble missionary he would make, —so sincere, so warm-hearted, so unselfish, so self-denying, so patient of labour, so uniformly cheerful, so wise and considerate, so self-possessed, so set upon exalting Christ and doing good to the souls of men! I believe this *tour* did much to strengthen in his mind his previous interest in the Highlands, the good effects of which are still felt in all the existing arrangements connected with this interesting region of our country.

V.

It was now the 20th day of August, and we were on our way to *Inverness*, where, on the following day, the General Assembly of the Free Church was to meet. This same General Assembly, when it closed its sittings in Edinburgh on June 3d, had adjourned to meet at *Inverness* (as set forth in the copy minute prefixed to this narrative), on August 21st, with the object of dealing specially with business affecting the Highlands. It was a great occasion for all the northern counties. Nothing of the kind had ever before been known in this region. The whole people were profoundly affected in prospect of what was to occur. An extensive migration commenced among them with the beginning of this week, and the tide of travellers flowed from every quarter towards the capital of the north.

We could conceive them, as they advanced, singing, each apart in their own tongue, in the spirit of the many thousands of Israel, when they gathered to their great annual festivals—

"I joy'd when to the house of God,
    Go up, they said to me.
Jerusalem, within thy gates
    Our feet shall standing be.
Jerusalem, as a city, is
    Compactly built together :

> Unto that place the tribes go up,
> The tribes of God go thither :
> " To Israel's testimony, there
> To God's name thanks to pay.
> For thrones of judgment, ev'n the thrones
> Of David's house, there stay."
>
> PSALM cxxii.

We travelled through the *Black Isle* and by KESSOCK Ferry. On our way we called at the Free manse of Ferintosh, hoping to see the worthy minister. He had gone to *Inverness.* So likewise had every person of note for whom we asked on our way, and we began to feel something of the impatience naturally caused by a fear, however groundless, that we might be too late.

When we arrived at Inverness, in the afternoon, we found the town in a state of great excitement. It was thronged with strangers, who had come from all quarters—men, women, and children. The prospect of the meeting of the General Assembly at *Inverness* had produced the strongest feeling of interest and delight all over the north. The northern counties, in every hamlet and in every cottage, were of the Free Church. None of the population who were Highlanders, had remained in the Established Church. The Disruption was felt to be a triumph of religious principle, and it was gloried in as being such. The MEN, as they are termed in this region, came flocking from the remotest districts, that they might be present at the meeting of the General Assembly—looking upon it and expecting it to be a great religious festival. The congregated multitudes were accustomed, both men and women, to vast gatherings at communion seasons—in such parishes particularly as that of Ferintosh ; but this *Assembly* was to be something beyond common gatherings,—a monster *gathering ;* and, with anticipations so great, the attraction was very strong. The multitudes who had crowded to *Inverness* were immense. The hospitality extended to them was unbounded ; so that, for the days during which our Supreme Court held its sittings, the *stir* was really oppressive.

The first friend whom I found out, or who rather searched for and found me, was Mr. Stewart of *Cromarty.* There was a special reason why we should take an interest of our own in the present condition of things at *Inverness.* Had there been nothing else than an early and long-continued friendship between us, this reason would have been enough to draw us together, and to make us inseparable for the days we were now to spend together here. After cordially greeting one another, and a few words about my tour in the west, he took my arm, and drew me to him, according to his old fashion, leading me along the street. It was crowded with persons dressed in the costumes usually worn, respectively, by the advanced in life of both sexes, moving slowly and demurely about, evidently big with expectation.

"Do you see these good creatures?" he said; "their notion of the Assembly meeting is, that it is to be a *big* sacrament,—such a sacrament as was never before in the north. If they don't get good preaching, and plenty of it, there will be disappointment."

It was delightful to mark the healthy, happy, nay, joyous countenances of ministers, elders, and others, convened on this occasion. The Highland ministers were decidedly in the majority, and masters of the situation, evidently anticipating a surprise to their southern brethren, many of whom, now in *Inverness*, had never before been to the north of the Grampians, and were very ignorant of the characteristics of the country and its inhabitants. The appearance of not a few of them presented a striking contrast to that of their northern friends. Many of them had performed the journey by sea, sailing from Leith on board the DUKE OF RICHMOND, a large steam-ship, which shortly afterwards was wrecked and went to pieces close to the pier of *Aberdeen*. On the journey they encountered dreadful weather, and were more than once in imminent peril. Their woe-begone aspect, on the evening which preceded the meeting of Assembly, too truly testified to the sufferings which they had endured, and the dangers to which they had been exposed.

The meeting-place of the Assembly was the *Academy Park*. There a huge wooden structure had been reared, and was fitted up, capable, as was estimated, of accommodating some 4000 persons, or even more. It was built in the style, and much after the plan, of the *Canonmills* Hall, and was fitted up internally much in the same way. The position of the Moderator's *chair*, the platform, the clerks' table, the bar, etc., was precisely the same. Mr. John Jaffrey (an official well known in the early days of the Free Church), who looked decidedly as if the *voyage* had done him no good, had brought with him the Canonmills *chair*, and one or two articles of furniture besides, which, in his opinion, were essential to the orderly procedure of the Supreme Court. Mr. Jaffrey was unrivalled in his appreciation of the outward proprieties requisite for an occasion so important as this great gathering in the ancient metropolis of the North Highlands, and his good efforts were duly valued. When the hour for the commencement of the services introductory to the opening of the Assembly arrived, the hall was filled to overflowing. Approaching the clerk's table on every side, the space was occupied by ministers, elders, and other office-bearers, the most distinguished of whom were seated on the platform. It was deeply interesting to notice the Highlanders in their home-manufactured and home-made costumes—the men in their hodden grey coats and cloaks; the women, some wearing the snow-white *mutch*, some the hair tastefully braided, as young women of the northern counties always braid it. The solemn, staid look of every one was so characteristic! It was such as I had often witnessed and admired at the monster communion meetings held on the hill-side, on the bright sacrament Sabbath days of bygone years. All were full of high expectation. They expected a "feast of fat things;" and on the first day, particularly, I think they had it.

Dr. Patrick Macfarlane of Greenock preached in *English* from EPHESIANS ii. 20-22—"Ye are built on the foundation of the apostles and prophets, Jesus Christ himself being the chief corner-stone; in whom all the building, fitly framed together, groweth unto an holy temple in the Lord; in whom ye also are builded together for an habitation of God through the Spirit." He conducted the whole service in this language, which was judiciously short, with his usual good taste and tact. The Highlanders, although he spoke in what was to many of them an unknown tongue, and although his voice did not nearly reach over the vast· area which they occupied, sat quietly and decorously until *their* turn. That came.

Dr. John M'Donald (the Apostle of the North), Moderator of this Assembly, preached and conducted all the services of the occasion in *Gaelic*. His text was Acts xvii. 6—" And when they found them not, they drew Jason and certain brethren unto the rulers of the city, crying, These that have turned the world upside down are come hither also."

Nothing could have been more politic nor better advised than this arrangement, and the effect was everything that could be desired. Never was the veteran " Apostle " in better heart for such work as that to which he was called on this occasion, and never were his ministrations more appropriate and acceptable.

The scene was striking. When he stood up in the pulpit (Dr. Macfarlane sitting beside him) to read the psalm in Gaelic, with the first notes of his voice the mighty mass, to its utmost verge—up to this time comparatively inanimate—at once seemed to become instinct with life. There was a moment's rustling as they all adjusted themselves in their seats, and then the sparkling of intelligent eyes, the unaffected deep emotion, the obvious secret prayer (without invitation) for the blessing to come down! Every line of the sweet song of praise, as it was read by lips which never spoke the gospel message but to delight his Highland hearers, seemed to thrill their hearts; every word in every line seemed to convey some happy, stirring idea to their expectant minds. Never have I seen the power of sympathy more strikingly illustrated or produce more hopeful effects. They all expected great things to be done in the midst of them.

Let us for a moment direct our attention to this remarkable man, the history of whose laborious and successful ministry has yet to be written, if it be ever done. He is before us in full vigour— his massive, robust, firmly-knit person, which has weathered the blasts of nearly *seventy* winters; his visage glowing and bronzed by the suns of as many summers—surmounted by the dark scanty wig, enclosing a head of finest mould; his clear black eye; his voice of sweetest melody—sweet and powerful, notwithstanding a life-long habit of enormous snuff-taking. Such was Dr. John M'Donald, the great Apostle of the North. Compare him with the amiable servant of God, Dr. Macfarlane, now by his side. No more striking contrast could be presented. In him we see the student of the cloister, with his ample brow and pale thin countenance; in the other the student of the highways and byeways, who has been in journeyings often, and in perils often—bearing the marks of it; the one nourished and enriched by stores of learning, on which he has luxuriated; the other made what he has become to the Church, not by culture, nor by any stores of knowledge other than the Scriptures, pure and simple, yield, and such as nature's child gathers from everything with which he becomes associated.

In whose hands the arrangements had been I know not; but they were admirably made to meet the tastes and religious feelings of my countrymen. The best Gaelic *precentor* of the north had been selected to lead the psalmody. He was a quiet-looking young man, about thirty years of age, of grave, but not of austere or pretentious aspect—dressed in the ordinary dress, the Sunday dress, of a farm servant—his hair brushed down on his brow—his ungloved hands, coarse and red with rustic toil—his demeanour modest, though quite self-possessed. He had faced assemblages as large before, although he had never sang in the presence of learned doctors or of fine gentlemen.

The first line of the psalm to be sung was read by the minister. The precentor chose one of the most plaintive and one of the sweetest of the *old long* tunes. Some voices joined in the music almost at the outset, as soon as they perceived what the tune selected was. When the precentor himself read the second line, in the grand style in which such precentors do read it, the burst of swelling melody which arose was magnificent and overwhelming. His voice extended everywhere, without any apparent effort. All heard, and all seemed to be fully qualified to join. Join they did; and, as one wave after another of vast harmonious sound rolled upon the ears of those who listened, but could not join, to judge from the expression of their countenances the effect was such as music had never produced on them before,—so touching, so sweet, so passing sweet. Friends from the south who had not before heard the *old* church tunes, with their beautiful prolonged variations, looked at each other for an instant, as if to say that now, for the first time, they were listening to the sound of praise as it ought always to be heard. Their looks were those of surprise—soon changed to looks expressive of the deepest emotion. Tears filled many eyes. Not a few, unable or unwilling to resist the tumult of their feelings, bent their heads forward on the book-boards, and wept, some audibly. · The prayer, and the sermon which followed, were such· as went to the hearts of all who understood the· language. And when the great congregation dis-· persed, it was very evident that the impression made had been great, edifying, and full of comfort.

During all the days of the Assembly the interest· was maintained, especially among the portion of the population who understood English. But I could· gather that the MEN, and those who were led by their opinion, were not satisfied that so much time was devoted to discussion and deliberation, and that so little, comparatively, was given to holy services. They did not understand that such discussion and deliberation were necessary, and that the Assembly had been convened chiefly for· this purpose. The idea of the "big sacrament" was predominant in their minds; and that· this should be interfered with, or even partially ignored, disappointed them. Dr. Chalmers, who had come in great financial power, to demonstrate the importance and excellence of the *Sustentation Fund*, and to urge its claims, though he made a most masterly statement, and addressed to them a very powerful appeal on his favourite topic, par-ticularly disappointed them. Indeed, our great

R

Leader never was, on such points, palatable to the Highlanders. Perhaps there is some truth in the allegation, though I am slow to admit it, that, do as you like, we Highlanders believe that we have a hereditary right to lay our burden on the Southerns, even when not unable to bear it ourselves.

I find among my notes written at this time, the following :—" The attendance in the immense pavilion provided was very great—by the lowest computation 4000 every day. The intermixture of Gaelic and English services, which was occasionally resorted to, had a happy effect. The superior. politeness of Highlanders to Lowlanders appeared. in this, that the former sat and listened as they best could, to what they did not understand, while the latter did not even make the attempt to follow their example. The Monday evening services were very brilliant. Dr. Buchanan of Glasgow, Mr. Begg, and Dr. Candlish, made three of the best continuous speeches I ever heard spoken in any Assembly."

Dr. Candlish's speech, on the refusal of sites for churches and manses by some of the Highland proprietors, has often been described as one of the most eloquent and effective he ever delivered. He was in fine health and in exuberant spirits. His heart's desire, I know, was to make the visit to INVERNESS productive of good to all the community of the northern counties. Aided by the noble band of men, who then surrounded and supported him, all of one heart and one mind, all, without one exception, aiming at the true prosperity and progress of our Zion, I believe he was, by God's blessing bestowed, made instrumental in effecting great good. All present seemed to breathe in a *revival* atmosphere.

Several ministers were present on this occasion who were not members of the Assembly, and who had no place in the discussions or deliberations of the time. But although this was so, such were not allowed to be out of sight, so far as it was regular to recognise them, and to make them available in the general cause. The favour was done me, for example, of inviting me to offer up one of the prayers, which were called for from time to time in the Assembly, besides being appointed to preach in one of the churches of the town. This duty I cheerfully undertook, and, I have reason to know, not without acceptance on the part of those to whom I preached—the explanation being simple.

At certain important points throughout the country, the ministers did not separate from the Establishment at the era of the Disruption, but continued to adhere to it. That was the case, to some extent, at *Inverness*. All the *quoad sacra* ministers joined the Free Church with their congregations, but the two ministers of the parochial charges did not. They both remained as they had been. They were the ministers of what was known as the ENGLISH *congregation*—a congregation intelligent, influential, and wealthy. Though the pastors had adopted this course, and though they were countenanced in it by the great bulk of their flock who abode with them, some were dissatisfied, and separated themselves,—making, as was customary in all such cases, application to the Supreme Court, or the committee appointed by the Supreme Court of the Free Church to deal with such cases, for aid in the shape of ministerial services. A very important part of the duty which devolved on our leading men, after the Assembly of 1843, was making arrangements and appointments to meet the necessities of such cases.

In this department of service all acknowledged there was no one to compare with Dr. Candlish. He seemed to have, almost intuitively, the most accurate conception of the condition of each locality from which the applications came. With this, he possessed, on the other hand, a wonderful acquaintance with the diversified gifts of almost all the ministers of our Church, so as to be able, as with the eye of a prophet, to single out the men suited to the service which required to be accomplished. It was such skill as gave to a leader, in such a crisis as that which led to the Disruption, a value of the kind which attaches to an accomplished commander of armies—it was a gift God provided, when the necessity for it arose.

The case of the *English* congregation in *Inverness* received ample consideration. The number who had separated, and who had made application for supply of ministerial service, was very small—a mere handful ; and, at the outset, but little coherence existed among them, and not much enthusiasm ; for never had separation from the Established Church been popular in the north. The order for *Inverness* in these circumstances was three months' continuous preaching and effort, by three ministers—not officiating at the same time, but succeeding each other—a fresh man being thus provided for each succeeding month for the allotted term. It was hoped that, by the end of that time, the congregation might be prepared to choose a pastor. The ministers named for this duty were *Mr. Beith* of Stirling, *Mr. Stewart* of Cromarty, and *Mr. Munro* of Rutherglen. The first month (July 1843) was mine ; the second (August) was Mr. Stewart's ; and the third (September) was Mr. Munro's. We were, of course, placed in communication with the local ecclesiastical authorities, with whom we were to consult and to co-operate.

Materials for a chapter, which might prove interesting, descriptive of the efforts which were made by the three deputies during these months, exist; but it is beside my purpose, in these pages, to go into details. Suffice it to say that these efforts—as the early records of the congregation will show—were signally successful; that, at the close of our term of service, the *English* Free Church congregation was organised, office-bearers were chosen and ordained, and all preliminary arrangements made for proceeding to call a minister; that soon thereafter a minister was accordingly called; and that, at this day, from beginnings so small, this congregation forms one of the most influential of the congregations of the Free Church—having enjoyed the benefit of the ministerial services of more than one of the most distinguished and honoured of her ministers.

Whilst I do not record the details of our three months' labours, I cannot refrain from inserting here, as I have before done elsewhere, some special notice of that singular man, one of the three deputies—now gone to his reward—who proved of such value at the time to which I refer—I mean Mr. STEWART of Cromarty.

VI.

A very intimate friendship was early (1817) established between Mr. Stewart and myself— a friendship which lasted without interruption through many years, until it pleased the good Lord to take him to himself. I never ceased to entertain for him the affection of a brother—a brother beloved.

The maturity of his mind, at this early period, was perhaps the most striking feature in his character. Though but a youth of little more than twenty, he seemed to possess the strong judgment and experience of a man of many years and of much reflection. I have been present in company with him when Dr. Love, and others of no ordinary powers, were of the party, and have heard him take part in conversation with them on difficult and deeply-interesting subjects, in such a manner as seemed at once greatly to surprise and gratify them. All felt, when he spoke, not merely from the modest demeanour which he manifested, but from the value and appropriateness of his observations, that he did not presume, and that he was entitled to take the place which he did. We were fellow-members of the Mnephilus (Preaching) Society, at that time including some very distinguished students. Discourses which he delivered in his turn to that Society, at our Saturday meetings in the College Church, Glasgow (the members scattering themselves over the whole extent of that old gaunt structure, getting into every remote corner, that the preacher for the day should be compelled to exert his voice, and make himself audible everywhere)—the same discourses which he delivered on these occasions, I have heard him deliver in after years, when he had become an ordained parish minister, to admiring and deeply-affected audiences in Edinburgh.

I had reason to know that on some occasions he used to try the acumen of Dr. Chalmers, whose warm friendship he enjoyed, with questions both in philosophy and theology, and that more than once he was put off with the half-sportive, half-evasive response, " Think of it, my dear sir."

It was well known at the time that, on Mr. Stewart's being licensed, Dr. Chalmers, after hearing him, was so impressed with his powers as a preacher, that he used every influence with him to gain his consent to be appointed his successor in the great church and parish of St. John's, from which he was about to be removed to St. Andrews. In this he was unquestionably right, considering Mr. Stewart's high talents, had his bodily constitution been equal to a burden so onerous. It was not so. His natural diffidence and self-distrust made him shrink from contemplating the proposal, or allowing it to become with him a matter of serious consideration at all; and I believe that the friends who knew him best, while they regretted the cause, entirely approved of the course which he adopted in the matter.

Distinguished though he always was, and eminent though he became at this early period of his life, no unworthy elation of mind was ever shown by him—no symptom whatever of undue self-esteem, of vanity, or of pride. The feeling predominant with him, I know, was hearty satisfaction, hearty self-gratulation at getting away from the public attention which he had drawn upon himself in Glasgow, and at being forgotten in relation to all the parochial arrangements which then excited in that city so much interest. Mr. Stewart was really a humble man, through the grace of God, of which he was the subject. For some part of this virtue in him, his natural good sense might account; for the whole, the indwelling of the Spirit could alone be a sufficient explanation.

I owe him much—very much. I have never ceased to reckon my association with him during my divinity course, and in the after years of my life, especially the earlier years of my ministry, as one of God's most gracious benefits bestowed on me. He was to me a wise and considerate guide in study — a guide whose counsel I thankfully received. He set before me clear, consistent, rich, and harmonious views of the great gospel doctrines, and thus greatly supplemented good Dr. M'Gill's prelections. He impressed my conscience (oh, how greatly was his own impressed!) with a deep sense of the awful responsibility of appearing as a public teacher to speak in the name of Christ—the responsibility not merely, and not chiefly, to the hearers to whom I might address myself, but the responsibility to Christ himself! What if He should say, "Who hath required this at your *hand?*"

In the light of such a consideration, he often spoke, in our long Saturday walks, many solemn words of the heavy moral obligation resting on us, in prospect of the ministry, to labour to be furnished for such a work, first by obtaining, through grace, the unction of the Holy Ghost, and then by possessing all the outward preparation which scriptural knowledge and theological acquirements generally implied—a preparation for the work of the ministry which could be secured only through earnest, patient, unremitting study, and much prayer. After I became a minister he greatly encouraged me. The following extract from a letter, written to me then, when he was still a student in the Hall, affords an illustration of this. He had just finished his "*Popular Discourse*" for Dr. M'Gill, to which he refers :—" Partly from the stiff, rusty state of my mind, and partly from reasons unknown, I could not get a comfortable grasp of my subject, and I had to turn it I don't know how many ways before I could get on at all. I am satisfied, however, that I have learned something by the discipline, although it does not appear in the sermon. When the burden pinched my own back, I was led to think of you, and to commit both to Him who is able to help. In this view some passages of Scripture forcibly occurred to my mind ; and I shall be happy if they afford you the same, or greater relief, according to your need, which they did to me—' Undertake for me, O Lord,' ' The Lord will provide.' He has provided an atoning sacrifice for us, He has provided a table in the wilderness richly furnished, He has provided a future rest—these things He has done ; but now, in respect of present and future difficulties, He will provide, and, *inter alia*, for the pulpit and the Sunday. A minister's preparation may be so poor as to be fitly compared to a few loaves and fishes ; but Christ's blessing can multiply it, not indeed into a luxurious feast, but a plain and plentiful meal. The loaves and the fishes were not miraculously created (Matt. xiv. 17), but were the property of the disciples. It was Christ's blessing on *what they had* that gave the increase. Jesus also gave first to the apostles, and they to the multitude. A minister then should not distress himself because he is deprived of the advantages of hearing the gospel, and because, like the priests, the Sabbath, instead of being a day of rest and enjoyment, is to him a day of anxiety and labour. Christ is His shepherd directly; he will receive his supply from Him piecemeal and in private; and what he thus receives, it will be his duty to distribute to his flock."

To the same effect is the following, written about the same time :—

"27th June 1821.

"You will ere now have commenced your labours. I shall be happy to know how you come on. I hope and earnestly pray that you may enjoy much of the Lord's blessing and countenance. The work is, no doubt, arduous, and obstacles and trials will be both numerous and severe. But this is just what we should expect, and lay our account with. Let us then fight, and labour, and suffer, as good soldiers. Our Almighty

Captain and King will not forsake us. New trials will entitle us to plead new promises, and will, I trust, afford us new proofs of His faithfulness. Who but the widow, the fatherless, the tempted, the oppressed, have a right to the promises made to persons in their peculiar circumstances? Being placed then, in a new situation, gives us a title to a new page in the Bible; we thus fall heirs to a new inheritance."

Mr. Stewart may have been to others all that, through God's blessing, I trust he was to me. I speak of my own experience only; and having an opportunity to bear a humble testimony to one whom I so well knew, I should feel that I had failed in duty did I not note these things of his youthful years, when as yet he had not become so fully known to the church, as in the subsequent years of his life.

His method of study afforded an example to be imitated. He had his fixed hours allotted to the various branches with which he was occupied. Nothing could induce him to break through this order. Nothing could induce him to relinquish his work until he had fulfilled his time, or completed his self-prescribed task. With a manly resolution, he on all occasions resisted any attempt which might be made, under whatever pretext, to cause him to swerve from his purpose. And thus he was able to have abundant time for necessary relaxation, as well as for required duty. His punctuality, as a result of this, was very exemplary. Never did he break an engagement, and never did he render a promise nugatory by delaying or by misplacing the performance of it.

With his deep and earnest piety Mr. Stewart had no austerity of character—no forbidding, affected, gloomy, morose seriousness of aspect and demeanour. In his case it was the very opposite ; this playfulness even of his usual manner, and its joyous hilarity on occasions, constituting to most persons an attractive feature in the form of his religious profession.

In stating these things of my early friend, I do not mean to assert that he was a favourite with all. There were those with whom he was no favourite. These were persons, however, who did not know him—persons to whom he gave no opportunity of knowing him—whom he rather delighted to keep in ignorance, though they might much desire to know him—and who therefore, naturally enough, betook themselves, perhaps in unconscious retaliation, to a dislike of him, which gave him no concern.

To speak the truth, he was not always amiable ; even to those who loved him and whom he loved. But they could easily bear with this ; indeed, after all, there was little to bear with. He soon, by his kind, conciliatory, and humble manner, obliterated every trace of unpleasant feeling, when such feeling had for a moment got footing in any loved one's mind.

Nothing more annoyed him than to be lionised. Even when a student, and particularly after he became a preacher, he was exposed to this. He could not away with it. An elderly lady whom he greatly respected, and who highly appreciated his excellences, whom he often edified, as well as delighted, by his conversation, lamenting that his " sweetness" should be " wasted" on her solitary self, resolved that she should make the attempt to share it with others. She engaged Mr. Stewart to take tea with her of an evening. Aware of his recluse habits, her party was to consist of only " one or two friends" whom he knew well. On his arrival at her house, however, he found a large assemblage of ladies, evidently on the tiptoe of anticipation. He was the only gentleman. The tea-drinking proceeded, and so did the universal talk usual on such occasions. Our friend spoke when addressed, and he told me, behaved, as he thought, to admiration. The tea things were removed in due time. Then various efforts were made by the kind hostess to exhibit her victim. They all failed. He was pleasant, and even jocose, but he was not what she desired. After some half-hour had thus passed, the whole party were shocked, when, as if rousing from a reverie, he suddenly stretched himself in his chair, and, with a half-wearied expression of voice and manner exclaimed, " I must away now and try to do some good," without further ceremony springing up, and, with his usual long heavy strides escaping out of the room. I was present next day when he received his rebuke from his well-meaning entertainer. As she went on to narrate the story to a greatly amused circle of friends, he got into fits of laughter. Every one present became infected. The offended lady could not herself resist his comical comments on the whole affair—comments which seemed even to justify his unpolite conduct. A free pardon, of course, followed, with a strong assurance from the kind lady that he would never again have from her the privilege of such an opportunity for doing good as he had so recklessly cast away.

It is somewhat strange to learn in this age of likeness-taking, when " likenesses," photographic and others, are almost as numerous as the population, that no likeness, no portrait of any sort, of Mr. Stewart, exists ; nothing to remind of his personal appearance those who knew him, or to inform those who knew him not. Being in Cromarty a short time after his death, I made inquiry, and ascertained the case to be so. I was indeed shown a thing cut out of black paper (it must have been done without Mr. Stewart's knowledge), which was called a likeness of him—but it bore no resemblance whatever to him. Had his picture ever been taken, it ought to have been as he appeared when occupied in the work of the sanctuary, "before the Lord," "and in the presence of all the people." May I add another to the sketches I have attempted in these pages?—

I see him enter the pulpit with a solemnity of aspect which is the fruit of real feeling. He is a tall, clumsily-made man, five feet eleven inches at least. The outline of his figure is more that of the female than the male. His limbs are full and round. There is a little tendency to stoop ; a little tendency, too, to corpulence, but very little. His chest is well thrown out, his shoulders somewhat raised, and his neck short. The head is a curiosity. It is nearly round, with a sort of wrench to one side. It rises high, being well developed in a circular arch above his ears, which are small and beautifully formed. It is covered with thick-set hair of a lightish sandy-colour, which invades the brow, covers the temples, and reaches to within an inch and a half of the eyebrows on all sides. Instead of being brushed down in the direction of its natural set, it is brushed up, to clear it off the short brow, and so stands, like a peak, at nearly right angles with the brow. The noble dimensions of that portion of the head are wholly concealed; and the effect on the beholder, at first sight, is to make him think that he is looking on one who must be a half-idiot. The eyebrows are not large nor expanded, but they rise a little at the extremities towards the temples. The nose is beautifully formed; large (but not too large), aquiline, and symmetrical, as if cut with the chisel. The eyes are small, grey, rather deep-set, sparkling, and expressive. The mouth is large; the line of the lips, which are thin, being beautifully curved. The lips shut easily, and look as if they had a superabundance of longitude. The chin is rather long, and is in a slight degree peaked, but is neither retiring nor protruding. The skin is as smooth as a lady's, and as destitute of all trace of beard, even of the down of early youth. The cheeks are not large. It is, taking it all in all, a handsome, though most uncommon head and face. I have never seen anything to compare with it.

Well, he enters the pulpit, and, after a moment's pause, rises to read the psalm. It is not a female voice, and yet it is not the rough voice of a man of his size and form. It is deep, clear, solemn, sweet, flexible, and of great compass. Every word is spoken as if the speaker felt himself standing in the presence of God, and in sight of the throne. The emphasis is so laid, in reading the psalm, as to bring out a meaning I had never discovered. His prayer is simplicity itself, a child can comprehend every word; yet his thoughts are of the richest; whilst Scripture phraseology, employed and applied as I never heard it in another, clothes them all. I have, by the time the prayer has ended, been instructed and edified. I have received views of truth I had not before, and have had feelings awakened which have set me on edge for the sermon, and which I desire to cherish for ever. The sermon comes. It seems to be a most deeply interesting and animated conversation on a common topic. "We ought to think like great men, and speak like the common people," appears to be the maxim which regulates the style. The manner is that of one who converses with a friend, and who has chosen a subject by the discussion of which he desires, from his inmost soul, to do him good. Illustration follows illustration in rapid succession, shedding light on and confirming his doctrine. Sometimes they seem puerile, scarcely dignified enough for the pulpit ; but that impression lasts only for a moment. Some Scripture allusion or Scripture quotation reveals the source from which they have been drawn, and I am filled with admiration of the genius which has discovered what I never discovered, and has made a use of it, which I think I and every man should naturally have made, but which I never did. Scarcely any gesture is employed. One hand rests usually on the open Bible ; the other is sometimes gently raised, and then its impressive short motion gives emphasis to the earnest words which are being spoken. The earnestness seems under severe control. It looks as if the speaker desired to conceal the emotion of his heart in speaking for Christ to sinners—as if he thought noise and gesticulation unbecoming. The eyelids get red, the tears apparently struggle to escape, but no tear comes. A pink spot, almost a hectic flush—but it is not so—appears like the reflection of an evening sunbeam on the cheek. Some burning words clothe some fine thought, which seems to have come fresh from heaven ; and the speaker, half ashamed, as I think, of the emotion which he has manifested, and which he has sensibly communicated to his hearers, returns to the calm manner from which he had for an instant departed, only, however, to be enticed from it again and again, yielding, as if by compulsion, to the inspiration which ever revisits him. So he proceeds, until, to your deep regret, he closes his wonderful sermon, which has extended long beyond the hour.

Mr. Stewart's local influence was great. Speeches by him in the Presbytery and Synod, were described by those who heard them as something unlike what any other man had ever spoken. On no occasion during his ministry did he open his mouth in the General Assembly. He did not feel it to be required. He did not think it would have been useful. All that he could say he heard spoken by others, and, as he thought, better spoken than it could have been by him, and therefore he did not speak. I by no means justify him in this. Could he have overcome his native timidity and want of self-possession, could he have roused himself to this effort, or had conscience impelled him to put himself forward as a public speaker, I believe he would not have stood second to any in the ranks of those wonderful men whom God raised up for his work in Scotland in his time. He believed that he could be useful in the provinces—that he was

required to take a part in the discussions there—
that the great cause might suffer if he declined to
do so; and therefore, on wisely-selected occasions
he delivered speeches that were admitted to be of
the very highest order of oratory—for wisdom,
beauty, and power.

When, in 1848, Dr. Candlish was, by appointment of the Church, to become one of the professors
in the New College, Edinburgh, Mr. Stewart was the
man to whom all eyes turned to succeed him in
St. George's. He shrank from it; the proposal
filled him with dismay. Friends urged him, and
after a long struggle, though believing at the same
time that he was about to offer himself to an early
death, he consented to accept the call.

Dr. Buchanan, of Glasgow, was one of the com-
missioners connected with the prosecution of the
call. When the business of the Presbytery had
ended, as they walked along the street, perceiving
the depressed appearance of his companion, he
expressed regret, saying, "You look as if you were
carrying a house upon your back." "No, Dr.
Buchanan," was the reply; "I am not carrying a
house, but I am carrying *my gravestone* on my back!"

I had been asked by friends in Edinburgh to use
my influence with him, and aid them in obtaining
his consent to the translation. I did write him,

though with many misgivings. I knew his bodily constitution, and feared the result of so great a change for him as a change from Cromarty to the metropolis. He wrote me, among other things, " I feel as if destitute of the faculties for dealing with *men*. I ought to have been a monk in a cloister, dealing with books and systems ; among living people I feel myself powerless as a child."

Soon after it was resolved to translate him he was taken with fever, brought on, it is much to be feared, by the excitement, and, to him, real affliction of the occasion. The fever soon ran its fatal course. He had little physical strength to resist it. The " inexorable minister of justice"—treading softly, however, and suppressing all triumph—speedily executed his commission, and the covenant-keeping Jehovah took away his faithful servant, in whom his grace had been so manifest, to the promised glory, and to his everlasting rest. " He got faith," said a valued friend who was much with him in the closing hours of life, " he got faith to lay his Isaac, bound, upon the altar ; his hand, in humble submission, took the knife ; he was prepared to do his Lord's will ; he did it ; and the Lord then relieved him for ever from all his cares, all his anxieties, and all his pains."

"Blessed saint! I shall think the more frequently of heaven that thou art there. I shall look more steadily toward the multitude of spirits of the righteous made perfect, because thou art one of them. And when, by the blood and righteousness of the Son of God, and by that mercy which is above the heavens, and which delivers from the lowest hell, the hour shall arrive of entrance into the high and holy place, amidst the astonishing solemnities and delights of that new situation, I shall soon look round to recognise thee, and to meet the sweetness of thy triumphant embrace."*
—*Dr. Love's Sermon on the Death of Dr. Balfour of Glasgow.*

* Such as are acquainted with the volume entitled THE TREE OF PROMISE, published in 1864, consisting of posthumous discourses by Mr. Stewart, will perceive that I have, in the foregoing sketch, made large use of what I have written there as a contribution to the biographical notice of my friend, prefixed to the volume. Although the work in question gives no adequate idea of the author's power as a preacher, having been compiled from meagre outlines used only in the pulpit, extended sometimes very imperfectly, yet I venture to say that the study of what may there be read will richly reward any one who resolves to occupy himself therewith. The student will find the discourses rich in original thought on Old Testament typology, and very precious as illustrating the fulness of evangelical truth taught in that typology. I should rejoice if anything I can say should have the effect of calling attention to THE TREE OF PROMISE—a work which, in my opinion, has never received the consideration to which it is entitled for its great merits.

VII.

When I undertook the work to be done at Inverness, my chief difficulty was the state of things at home, the yet chaotic condition of my own flock, and consequently the risks connected with my leaving them, so soon after the great change at the Disruption, for a whole month. As in duty bound, I stated this difficulty at the conference in Edinburgh, when all the arrangements for the Church at large, as I have already intimated, were made.

" If I could be assured of satisfactory supply for my pulpit during my absence," I said, " I should feel little difficulty in agreeing to the proposal that I shall take the first month at Inverness."

Various suggestions were made, and supply by one or two esteemed clerical friends was offered.

" I'll give you a day," said Dr. Candlish, after a little. " Will that satisfy you ?"—" It will," I answered ; " and if you make your day towards the close of the month, the expectation of your visit will keep all pleasant till you come."

This was agreed to ; other appointments were made and noted, and I felt my way made plain.

The FREE NORTH CHURCH congregation, Stirling, worshipped for the first year in the CORN

EXCHANGE there—a long, narrow, but withal commodious building, high roofed, ornamented with various devices in the ceiling, comfortably floored, well lighted, and, from the multiplicity of doors, well ventilated. To my unspeakable surprise, when I came from Edinburgh on the Saturday evening before the second Sabbath after the Disruption, as it was arranged all the Free Church ministers should do, to preach at home to those who followed them, I found the CORN EXCHANGE fitted up as a place of worship for my flock. Benches were placed on the floor, nearly to its utmost extremity, and a well-constructed pulpit was just being decorated with green velvet, the gift of one of the ladies of the flock, as I was conducted into the building to see the preparations made for the morrow. There I preached next day to a " full house," a very large gathering, such as I had by no means expected. There I continued to preach until the month of April 1844 ; and there, I may be forgiven for adding, I realised the *ideal* of a really *free* congregation—*free sittings,* full liberty for all, of every name, to come and go ; no allocation of sittings, no rents for sittings ; the expense of all service, rent, etc., borne by collections made at the doors, and no unnecessary formalities of any kind. I confess that, when we passed

into the subsequent order of things, there was a
difference. Paul "for two whole years," in "his
own *hired* house," at Rome, "received all that
came in unto him, preaching to them." We for one
year had our worship and services of a similar kind
in our "*hired*" house. Could there not be some
system of arrangement by which in *hired* places
the good work might be carried on? What vexing
questions as to Church property, and other legal
entanglements, might not in this way be prevented!

In the CORN EXCHANGE, when he came, Dr.
Candlish preached. During our great controversy,
and before our liberty was achieved, he often spoke
of the relief which he expected to experience when
the conflict should be all past, whatever the cost
might be, and when he should be free to give himself to the preaching of the glorious gospel, going
everywhere to do so without let or hindrance. Such
as had the happiness to hear him preach when
the time of liberty came, know how much this was
realised in his unwearied efforts, his burning zeal,
and his most powerful appeals to the hearts and
consciences of men.

The CORN EXCHANGE was filled to overflowing
to hear him—a congregation formed without respect
to denomination or locality. Of every name, and
from all the neighbourhood, the people were

gathered to hear him. Twice, forenoon and afternoon, he preached with great animation.

He had spoken to my wife of his desire to preach
somewhere in the country, in the open air, in the
evening. Thinking that it might overtask his
strength, and believing that he required repose, she
tried to dissuade him. But no ; he should like it
so much ; and, of all places, " somewhere on the
slopes of the OCHILS ;"—on the east of the GRAMPIAN
range, some five miles to the north of Stirling.
Accordingly he gave notice, at the close of both
services in the Corn Exchange, of his intention,
making request that, if possible, intimation might
be sent to the locality. The intimation soon took
wing. There were earnest spirits among my flock,
who charged themselves with the duty of making
known in all the villages at " the foot of the hills,"
that Dr. Candlish was to preach on the OCHILS,
as well as the expected *whereabouts* of his proposed
service.

At dinner he was in great spirits—happy in
review of the work already done, and happy in
anticipation of what was in prospect.

" You'll go with me ?" he said to my wife ;
" I will drive you myself. We shall have an open
conveyance." The day was one of the broiling days
under which I was suffering at Inverness.

" Yes, indeed I will go with you," was the answer.

In due time the conveyance, a *gig*, came to the door.

" Had you not better allow the boy" (who had brought the conveyance) " to drive? He will be acquainted with the horse?"

" Oh, I can drive quite well myself. Come away, and you will judge of my skill and ability," he said, with his usual happy laugh.

He was cautious in descending our steep streets. We then lived near the Castle. Once on level ground he seemed to think caution not so necessary a virtue. Away they went. My wife told me afterwards that she looked for an upset, or something untoward. Nothing of the kind occurred. Over the hill at AIRTHREY they went at a lively pace, other vehicles following, down into the beautiful valley below. The assembled multitude at length came in sight. The hour of service had arrived. There were ready hands to care for the horse. But slight accommodation was made for the preacher—a table and a chair. The audience, which was very great, were seated on the mountain-side, in front and on each side of him. It was truly an out-of-door mountain evangelical service. The people, many of them, were greatly affected. In after years the circumstance was often talked of, and oftentimes have I had the details given to me by sundry hearers on the occasion.

The service concluded, Dr. Candlish resumed the office of driver; and in perfect safety, and to the perfect satisfaction of all interested, arrived at his resting-place for the night. Next day, as soon as he had breakfasted, he was off and away, to undertake other duty in some other place in behalf of some other brother in the same cause.

I have had several tours with Dr. Candlish—all of them very interesting to me. But if the notes I have recorded of them shall ever see the light, it must be under other editorship than mine, for friends, *who still survive*, were associated with us. Of them I could not be free to speak as I should like to do *now*. And I am not to suppose, to expect, or to desire, that any future shall afford *me* the opportunity as to them which I possess with regard to him who is no longer with us— who has gone " to the mountain of myrrh, and to the hill of frankincense," there to abide " until the day break, and the shadows flee away."

" And what's a life ? a weary pilgrimage,
  Whose glory in one day doth fill thy stage
  With childhood, manhood, and decrepit age.

" And what's a life ? the flourishing array
Of the proud summer meadow, which to-day
Wears her green plush, and is to-morrow hay."

Francis Quarles.

THE END.

Printed by R. & R. CLARK, *Edinburgh.*